# Devils Devils Devils

# Devils Devils Devils

Selected by HELEN HOKE

Pictures by
CAROL BARKER

FRANKLIN WATTS | NEW YORK | LONDON | 1976

# CONTENTS

# acknowledgments

The selections in this book are used by permission and special arrangements with the proprietors of their respective copyrights, who are listed below. The editor's and publisher's thanks go to all who made this collection possible.

The editor and publisher have made every effort to trace ownership of all material contained herein. It is their belief that the necessary permissions from publishers, authors, and authorized agents have been obtained in all cases. In the event of any questions arising as to the use of any material, the editor and publisher express regret for any error unconsciously made and will be pleased to make the necessary correction in future editions of the book.

"The Boots That Never Wore Out", reprinted by permission of Coward, McCann & Geoghegan, Inc., from *13 Devils*, by Dorothy Gladys Spicer. Copyright © 1967 by Dorothy Gladys Spicer.

"Yann the Fearless", from *Folktales of France*, ed. G. Massignon, 1968. Reprinted by permission of the University of Chicago Press. © 1968 by the University of Chicago.

"The Devil in the Churchyard", from *The Black Dog*, by A. E. Coppard. Reprinted by permission of Jonathan Cape, Ltd. and the Estate of A. E. Coppard.

"The Devil", by Guy de Maupassant, from *The Complete Stories of Guy de Maupassant*, published by Hanover House, 1955.

ACKNOWLEDGMENTS

"How the Devil Married Three Sisters", reprinted from *One Hundred Favorite Folktales*, by Stith Thompson. © 1968 Indiana University Press, Bloomington. Reprinted by permission of the publisher.

"The Stolen Heart", from *The Wily Wizard and the Wicked Witch*, by Godfried Bomans. English translation copyrighted by J. M. Dent & Sons, Ltd., London, 1969, and Franklin Watts, Inc., New York, 1969.

"The Smith and the Devil", by Frederick W. Robins, from *The Smith*. Reprinted by permission of Rider & Co., London.

"The Demon and the Rabbi", by M. A. Jagendorf, from *Ghostly Folktales*, by M. A. Jagendorf. © General Learning Corporation. Reprinted by permission.

"The Devil and Daniel Webster", from *The Selected Works of Stephen Vincent Benet*. Copyright, 1936, by the Curtis Publishing Company. Copyright renewed © 1964 by Thomas C. Benet, Stephanie B. Mahin, and Rachel B. Lewis. Reprinted by permission of Brandt & Brandt.

"Witches' Hollow", by H. P. Lovecraft and August Derleth, from *The Shuttered Window*. Reprinted by permission of the August Derleth Estate.

# ABOUT THIS BOOK

Devils are popular figures in folklore stories; like giants, dragons and witches, they inhabit every country in the world. Very often the same devil story will be found in several different countries; it is the telling of it that gives each version its own regional flavour. In this selection I have included devils from France, Finland, Italy, Belgium, the Philippines, Great Britain and the U.S.A. There are even an ancient rabbinical story, and an old Welsh gypsy folktale.

Devils have been around since time immemorial! According to folklore, there is not just one devil—Satan, the enemy of God—but all kinds of lesser devils as well; evil spirits or heathen gods. These devils are traditionally wicked and crafty—but, as in all folktales, good overcomes evil, and the devils are usually outwitted.

In the Finnish folktale, young Jussi outwits the Devil in a series of confrontations and frees Finland of devils forever. From France, Yann the Fearless frees a king's daughter from her fate with the Devil; and in the Filippino tale, Piriang and her mother see through the Devil's disguise. But Daniel Webster, in *The Devil and Daniel Webster*, is up against the toughest of them all! This superb story tells how Webster wins a fight with the Devil only by using his lawyer's eloquence.

Even devils can be human, as we discover in *The Stolen Heart*, where the devil has compassion for the poor fisherman's son.

But crafty or compassionate, it is generally agreed that devils are frightening creatures. The old washerwoman plays on this fact in Guy de Maupassant's amusing story; so does brother Mark in A. E. Coppard's *Devil in the Churchyard*.

One of the interesting facts which emerged from reading lots of devil stories was that the favourite method of catching devils seems to have been in a bottle. Piriang and her mother imprison the devil in a large bottle in *The Devil and the Guachinango*; and in Robert Louis Stevenson's marvellous story an imp is imprisoned in a bottle of unbreakable glass, tempered in Hell! Even though he is trapped, this devil still gets his victim!

I hope you enjoy reading this collection of devilry as much as I did amassing it.

*Helen Hoke*

# Devils Devils Devils

# THE BOTTLE IMP

## ROBERT LOUIS STEVENSON

*In which Keawe buys a strange bottle with an imp imprisoned inside it. The glass is unbreakable, for it was tempered in the flames of Hell! If any man buys the bottle, the imp is at his command; all that he desires— love, fame, money—are his at the word uttered. But there is one drawback: if a man dies before he sells the bottle, he must burn in Hell forever . . .*

THERE WAS a man of the island of Hawaii, whom I shall call Keawe; for the truth is, he still lives, and his name must be kept secret; but the place of his birth was not far from Honaunau, where the bones of Keawe the Great lie hidden in a cave. This man was poor, brave, and active; he could read and write like a schoolmaster; he was a first-rate mariner besides, sailed for some time in the island steamers, and steered a whaleboat on the Hamakua coast. At length it came in Keawe's mind to have a sight of the great world and foreign cities, and he shipped on a vessel bound to San Francisco.

This is a fine town, with a fine harbour, and rich people uncountable; and, in particular, there is one hill covered with palaces. Upon this hill Keawe was one day taking a walk with his pocket full of money, viewing the great houses upon either hand with pleasure. "What fine houses there are!" he was thinking, "and how happy must those people be who dwell in them, and take no care for the morrow!" The thought was in his mind when he came abreast of a house that was smaller than some others, but all finished and beautified like a toy; the steps of that house shone like silver, and the borders of the garden bloomed like garlands, and the windows were bright like diamonds; and Keawe stopped and wondered at the excellence of all he saw. So stopping, he was aware of a man that looked forth upon him through a window so clear that Keawe could see him as you see a fish in a pool upon the reef. The man was elderly, with a bald head and a black beard; and his face was heavy with sorrow, and he bitterly sighed. And the truth of it is, that as Keawe looked in upon the man, and the man looked out upon Keawe, each envied the other.

All of a sudden the man smiled and nodded, and beckoned Keawe to enter, and met him at the door of the house.

"This is a fine house of mine," said the man, and bitterly sighed. "Would you not care to view the chambers?"

So he led Keawe all over it, from the cellar to the roof, and there was nothing there that was not perfect of its kind, and Keawe was astonished.

"Truly," said Keawe, "this is a beautiful house; if I lived in the like of it, I should be laughing all day long. How comes it, then, that you should be sighing?"

"There is no reason," said the man, "why you should not have a house in all points similar to this, and finer, if you wish. You have some money, I suppose?"

"I have fifty dollars," said Keawe; "but a house like this will cost more than fifty dollars."

The man made a computation. "I am sorry you have no more," said he, "for it may raise you trouble in the future; but it shall be yours at fifty dollars."

"The house?" asked Keawe.

"No, not the house," replied the man; "but the bottle. For, I must tell you, although I appear to you so rich and fortunate, all my fortune, and this house itself and its garden, came out of a bottle not much bigger than a pint. This is it."

And he opened a lockfast place, and took out a round-bellied bottle with a long neck; the glass of it was white like milk, with changing rainbow colours in the grain. Within-sides something obscurely moved, like a shadow and a fire.

"This is the bottle," said the man; and when Keawe laughed, "You do not believe me?" he added. "Try, then, for yourself. See if you can break it."

So Keawe took the bottle up and dashed it on the floor till he was weary; but it jumped on the floor like a child's ball and was not injured.

"This is a strange thing," said Keawe. "For by the

touch of it, as well as by the look, the bottle should be of glass."

"Of glass it is," replied the man, sighing more heavily than ever; "but the glass of it was tempered in the flames of hell. An imp lives in it, and that is the shadow we behold there moving; or so I suppose. If any man buy this bottle the imp is at his command; all that he desires—love, fame, money, houses like this house, ay, or a city like this city—all are his at the word uttered. Napoleon had this bottle, and by it he grew to be the king of the world; but he sold it at the last, and fell. Captain Cook had this bottle, and by it he found his way to so many islands; but he, too, sold it, and was slain upon Hawaii. For, once it is sold, the power goes and the protection; and unless a man remain content with what he has, ill will befall him."

"And yet you talk of selling it yourself?" Keawe said.

"I have all I wish, and I am growing elderly," replied the man. "There is one thing the imp cannot do—he cannot prolong life; and, it would not be fair to conceal from you, there is a drawback to the bottle; for if a man die before he sells it, he must burn in hell for ever."

"To be sure, that is a drawback and no mistake," cried Keawe. "I would not meddle with the thing. I can do without a house, thank God; but there is one thing I could not be doing with one particle, and that is to be damned."

"Dear me, you must not run away with things," returned the man. "All you have to do is to use the power of the imp in moderation, and then sell it to someone else, as I do to you, and finish your life in comfort."

"Well, I observe two things," said Keawe. "All the time you keep sighing like a maid in love, that is one; and, for the other, you sell this bottle very cheap."

"I have told you already why I sigh," said the man. "It is because I fear my health is breaking up; and, as you said yourself, to die and go to the devil is a pity for anyone. As for why I sell so cheap, I must explain to you there is a peculiarity about the bottle. Long ago, when the devil brought it first upon earth, it was extremely expensive, and was sold first of all to Prester John for many millions of dollars; but it cannot be sold at all, unless sold at a loss. If you sell it for as much as you paid for it, back it comes to you again like a homing pigeon. It follows that the price has kept falling in these centuries, and the bottle is now remarkably cheap. I bought it myself from one of my great neighbours on this hill, and the price I paid was only ninety dollars. I could sell it for as high as eighty-nine dollars and ninety-nine cents, but not a penny dearer, or back the thing must come to me. Now, about this there are two bothers. First, when you offer a bottle so singular for eighty-odd dollars, people suppose you to be jesting. And second—but there is no hurry about that—and I need not go into it. Only remember it must be *coined* money that you sell it for."

"How am I to know that this is all true?" asked Keawe.

"Some of it you can try at once," said the man. "Give me your fifty dollars, take the bottle, and wish your fifty dollars back into your pocket. If that does not happen, I pledge you my honour I will cry off the bargain and restore your money."

"You are not deceiving me?" said Keawe.

The man bound himself with a great oath.

"Well, I will risk that much," said Keawe, "for that can do no harm." And he paid over his money to the man, and the man handed him the bottle.

"Imp of the bottle," said Keawe, "I want my fifty dollars back." And sure enough he had scarce said the word before his pocket was as heavy as ever.

"To be sure, this is a wonderful bottle," said Keawe.

"And now good morning to you, my fine fellow, and the devil go with you for me!" said the man.

"Hold on," said Keawe, "I don't want any more of this fun. Here, take your bottle back."

"You have bought it for less than I paid for it," replied the man, rubbing his hands. "It is yours now; and, for my part, I am only concerned to see the back of you." And with that he rang for his Chinese servant, and had Keawe shown out of the house.

Now, when Keawe was in the street, with the bottle under his arm, he began to think, "If all is true about this bottle, I may have made a losing bargain," thinks he. "But perhaps the man was only fooling me." The first thing he did was to count his money; the sum was exact—forty-nine dollars American money, and one

Chili piece. "That looks like the truth," said Keawe. "Now I will try another part."

The streets in that part of the city were as clean as a ship's deck, and though it was noon, there were no passengers. Keawe set the bottle in the gutter and walked away. Twice he looked back, and there was the milky, round-bellied bottle where he left it. A third time he looked back and turned a corner; but he had scarce done so, when something knocked upon his elbow, and behold! it was the long neck sticking up; and as for the round belly, it was jammed into the pocket of his pilot-coat.

"And that looks like the truth," said Keawe.

The next thing he did was to buy a corkscrew in a shop, and go apart into a secret place in the fields. And there he tried to draw the cork, but as often as he put the screw in, out it came again, and the cork as whole as ever.

"This is some new sort of cork," said Keawe, and all at once he began to shake and sweat, for he was afraid of that bottle.

On his way back to the port-side he saw a shop where a man sold shells and clubs from the wild islands, old heathen deities, old coined money, pictures from China and Japan, and all manner of things that sailors bring in their sea-chests. And here he had an idea. So he went in and offered the bottle for a hundred dollars. The man of the shop laughed at him at the first, and offered him five; but, indeed, it was a curious bottle—

such glass was never blown in any human glass-works, so prettily the colours shone under the milky white, and so strangely the shadows hovered in the midst; so, after he had disputed a while after the manner of his kind, the shopman gave Keawe sixty silver dollars for the thing, and set it on a shelf in the midst of his window.

"Now," said Keawe, "I have sold that for sixty which I bought for fifty—or, to say truth, a little less, because one of my dollars was from Chili. Now I shall know the truth upon another point."

So he went back on board his ship, and, when he opened his chest, there was the bottle, and had come more quickly than himself. Now Keawe had a mate on board whose name was Lopaka.

"What ails you," said Lopaka, "that you stare in your chest?"

They were alone in the ship's forecastle, and Keawe bound him to secrecy, and told all.

"This is a very strange affair," said Lopaka, "and I fear you will be in trouble about this bottle. But there is one point very clear—that you are sure of the trouble, and you had better have the profit in the bargain. Make up your mind what you want with it; give the order, and if it is done as you desire, I will buy the bottle myself; for I have an idea of my own to get a schooner, and go trading through the islands."

"That is not my idea," said Keawe; "but to have a beautiful house and garden on the Kona coast, where

I was born, the sun shining in at the door, flowers in the garden, glass in the windows, pictures on the walls, and toys and fine carpets on the tables, for all the world like the house I was in this day—only a storey higher, and with balconies all about like the King's Palace; and to live there without care and make merry with my friends and relatives."

"Well," said Lopaka, "let us carry it back with us to Hawaii; and if all comes true, as you suppose, I will buy the bottle, as I said, and ask a schooner."

Upon that they were agreed, and it was not long before the ship returned to Honolulu, carrying Keawe and Lopaka, and the bottle. They were scarce come ashore when they met a friend upon the beach, who began at once to condole with Keawe.

"I do not know what I am to be condoled about," said Keawe.

"Is it possible you have not heard," said the friend, "your uncle—that good old man—is dead, and your cousin—that beautiful boy—was drowned at sea?"

Keawe was filled with sorrow, and beginning to weep and lament, he forgot about the bottle. But Lopaka was thinking to himself and, presently, when Keawe's grief was a little abated, "I have been thinking," said Lopaka. "Had not your uncle lands in Hawaii, in the district of Kau?"

"No," said Keawe, "not in Kaü; they are on the mountainside—a little way south of Hookena."

"These lands will now be yours?" asked Lopaka.

"And so they will," said Keawe, and began again to lament for his relatives.

"No," said Lopaka, "do not lament at present. I have a thought in my mind. How if this should be the doing of the bottle? For here is the place ready for your house."

"If this be so," cried Keawe, "it is a very ill way to serve me by killing my relatives. But it may be, indeed; for it was in just a place that I saw the house with my mind's eye."

"The house, however, is not yet built," said Lopaka.

"No, nor like to be!" said Keawe, "for though my uncle has some coffee and ava and bananas, it will not be more than will keep me in comfort; and the rest of that land is the black lava."

"Let us go to the lawyer," said Lopaka, "I have still this idea in my mind."

Now, when they came to the lawyer's, it appeared Keawe's uncle had grown monstrous rich in the last days, and there was a fund of money.

"And here is the money for the house!" cried Lopaka.

"If you are thinking of a new house," said the lawyer, "here is the card of a new architect, of whom they tell me great things."

"Better and better!" cried Lopaka. "Here is all made plain for us. Let us continue to obey orders."

So they went to the architect, and he had drawings of houses on his table.

"You want something out of the way," said the

architect. "How do you like this?" and he handed a drawing to Keawe.

Now, when Keawe set eyes on the drawing, he cried out aloud, for it was the picture of his thought exactly drawn.

"I am in for this house," thought he. "Little as I like the way it comes to me, I am in for it now, and I may as well take the good along with the evil."

So he told the architect all that he wished, and how he would have the house furnished, and about the pictures on the wall and the knick-knacks on the tables; and he asked the man plainly for how much he would undertake the whole affair.

The architect put many questions, and took his pen and made a computation; and when he had done he named the very sum that Keawe had inherited.

Lopaka and Keawe looked at one another and nodded.

"It is quite clear," thought Keawe, "that I am to have this house, whether or no. It comes from the devil, and I fear I will get little good by that; and of one thing I am sure, I will make no more wishes as long as I have this bottle. But with the house I am saddled, and I may as well take the good along with the evil."

So he made his terms with the architect, and they signed a paper; and Keawe and Lopaka took ship again and sailed to Australia; for it was concluded between them that they should not interfere at all, but leave the architect and the bottle imp to build and to adorn that house at their own pleasure.

The voyage was a good voyage, only all the time Keawe was holding in his breath, for he had sworn he would utter no more wishes, and take no more favours from the devil. The time was up when they got back. The architect told them that the house was ready, and Keawe and Lopaka took a passage in the *Hall*, and went down Kona way to view the house, and see if all had been done fitly according to the thought that was in Keawe's mind.

Now, the house stood on the mountainside, visible to ships. Above, the forest ran up into the clouds of rain; below, the black lava fell in cliffs, where the kings of old lay buried. A garden bloomed about that house with every hue of flowers; and there was an orchard of papais on the one hand and an orchard of bread-fruit on the other, and right in front, toward the sea, a ship's mast had been rigged up and bore a flag. As for the house, it was three storeys high, with great chambers and broad balconies on each. The windows were of glass, so excellent that it was as clear as water and as bright as day. All manner of furniture adorned the chambers. Pictures hung upon the wall in golden frames; pictures of ships, and men fighting, and of the most beautiful women, and of singular places; nowhere in the world are there pictures of so bright a colour as those Keawe found hanging in his house. As for knick-knacks, they were extraordinarily fine; chiming clocks and musical boxes, little men with nodding heads, books filled with pictures, weapons of price from all quarters of the world, and the most elegant puzzles to entertain the leisure of a solitary man. As no one would care to live in such chambers, only to walk through them and view them, the balconies were made so broad that a whole town might have lived upon them in delight; and Keawe knew not which to prefer, whether the back porch, where you got the land-breeze, and looked upon the orchards and the flowers, or the front balcony, where you could drink the wind of the sea, and look down the steep wall of the mountain and see the *Hall* going by once a week or so between Hookena and the hills of Pele, or the schooners plying up the coast for wood and ava and bananas.

When they had viewed all, Keawe and Lopaka sat on the porch.

"Well," asked Lopaka, "is it all as you designed?"

"Words cannot utter it," said Keawe. "It is better than I dreamed, and I am sick with satisfaction."

"There is but one thing to consider," said Lopaka; "all this may be quite natural and the bottle imp have nothing whatever to say to it. If I were to buy the bottle, and got no schooner after all, I should have put my hand in the fire for nothing. I gave you my word, I know; but yet I think you would not grudge me one more proof."

"I have sworn I would take no more favours," said Keawe. "I have gone already deep enough."

"This is no favour I am thinking of," replied Lopaka. "It is only to see the imp himself. There is nothing to be gained by that; and so nothing to be ashamed of; and yet, if I once saw him, I should be sure of the whole matter. So indulge me so far, and let me see the imp; and, after that, here is the money in my hand, and I will buy it."

"There is only one thing I am afraid of," said Keawe. "The imp may be very ugly to view: and if once you set eyes on him you might be very undesirous of the bottle."

"I am a man of my word," said Lopaka. "And here is the money betwixt us."

"Very well," replied Keawe. "I have a curiosity myself. So come, let us have one look at you, Mr. Imp."

Now as soon as that was said the imp looked out of the bottle, and in again, swift as a lizard; and there sat Keawe and Lopaka turned to stone. The night had quite come before either found a thought to say or voice to say it with; and then Lopaka pushed the money over and took the bottle.

"I am a man of my word," said he, "and had need to be so, or I would not touch this bottle with my foot. Well, I shall get my schooner and a dollar or two for my pocket; and then I will be rid of this devil as fast as I can. For to tell you the plain truth, the look of him has cast me down."

"Lopaka," said Keawe, "do not you think any worse of me than you can help; I know it is night, and the roads bad, and the pass by the tombs an ill place to go by so late, but I declare since I have seen that little face, I cannot eat or sleep or pray till it is gone from me. I will give you a lantern, and a basket to put the bottle in, and any picture or fine thing in all my house that takes your fancy—and be gone at once, and go to sleep at Hookena with Nahinu."

"Keawe," said Lopaka, "many a man would take this ill; above all, when I am doing you a turn so friendly as to keep my word and buy the bottle; and for that matter, the night, and the dark, and the way by the tombs, must be all tenfold more dangerous to a man with such a sin upon his conscience, and such a bottle under his arm. But for my part, I am so extremely terrified myself, I have not the heart to blame you. Here I go then; and I pray God you may be happy in your house, and I fortunate with my schooner, and both get to heaven in the end in spite of the devil and his bottle."

So Lopaka went down the mountain; and Keawe stood in his front balcony, and listened to the clink of the horse's shoes, and watched the lantern go shining down the path, and along the cliff of caves where the old dead are buried; and all the time he trembled and clasped his hands, and prayed for his friend, and gave glory to God that he himself was escaped out of that trouble.

*   *   *

But the next day came very brightly, and that new house of his was so delightful to behold that he forgot his terrors. One day followed another, and Keawe dwelt there in perpetual joy. He had his place on the back porch; it was there he ate and lived, and read the stories in the Honolulu newspapers; but when any one came by they would go in and view the chambers and the pictures. And the fame of the house went far and wide; it was called *Ka-Hale-Nui*—the Great House— in all Kona; and sometimes the Bright House, for Keawe kept a Chinaman, who was all day dusting and furbishing; and the glass, and the gilt, and the fine stuffs, and the pictures, shone as bright as the morning. As for Keawe himself, he could not walk in the chambers without singing, his heart was so enlarged; and when ships sailed by upon the sea, he would fly his colours on the mast.

So time went by, until one day Keawe went upon a visit as far as Kailua to certain of his friends. There he was well feasted; and left as soon as he could the next morning, and rode hard, for he was impatient to behold his beautiful house; and, besides, the night then coming on was the night in which the dead of old days go abroad in the sides of Kona; and having already meddled with the devil, he was the more chary of meeting with the dead. A little beyond Honaunau, looking far ahead, he was aware of a woman bathing in the edge of the sea; and she seemed a well-grown girl, but he thought no more of it. Then he saw her white shift flutter as she put it on, and then her red holoku; and by the time he came abreast of her she was done with her toilet, and had come up from the sea, and stood by the track side in her red holoku, and she was all freshened with the bath, and her eyes shone and were kind. Now Keawe no sooner beheld her than he drew rein.

"I thought I knew everyone in this country," said he. "How comes it that I do not know you?"

"I am Kokua, daughter of Kiano," said the girl, "and I have just returned from Oahu. Who are you?"

"I will tell you who I am in a little," said Keawe, dismounting from his horse, "but not now. For I have a thought in my mind, and if you knew who I was, you might have heard of me, and would not give me a true answer. But tell me, first of all, one thing: are you married?"

At this Kokua laughed out aloud. "It is you who ask questions," she said. "Are you married yourself?"

"Indeed, Kokua, I am not," replied Keawe, "and never thought to be until this hour. But here is the plain truth. I have met you here at the roadside, and I saw your eyes, which are like the stars, and my heart went to you as swift as a bird. And so now, if you want none of me, say so, and I will go on to my own place; but if you think me no worse than any other young man, say so, too, and I will turn aside to your father's for the night, and tomorrow I will talk with the good man."

Kokua said never a word, but she looked at the sea and laughed.

"Kokua," said Keawe, "if you say nothing, I will take that for the good answer; so let us be stepping to your father's door."

She went on ahead of him, still without speech; only sometimes she glanced back and glanced away again, and she kept the strings of her hat in her mouth.

Now, when they came to the door, Kiano came out on his verandah, and cried out and welcomed Keawe by name. At that the girl looked over, for the fame of the great house had come to her ears; and, to be sure, it was a great temptation. All that evening they were very merry together; and the girl was as bold as brass under the eyes of her parents, and made a mock of Keawe, for she had a quick wit. The next day he had a word with Kiano, and found the girl alone.

"Kokua," said he, "you made a mock of me all the evening; and it is still time to bid me go. I would not tell you who I was, because I have so fine a house, and I feared you would think too much of that house and too little of the man that loves you. Now you know all, and if you wish to have seen the last of me, say so at once."

"No," said Kokua; but this time she did not laugh, nor did Keawe ask for more.

This was the wooing of Keawe; things had gone quickly; but so an arrow goes, and the ball of a rifle swifter still, and yet both may strike the target. Things had gone fast, but they had gone far also, and the thought of Keawe rang in the maiden's head; she heard his voice in the breach of the surf upon the lava, and for this young man that she had seen but twice she would have left her father and mother and her native islands. As for Keawe himself, his horse flew up the path of the mountain under the cliff of tombs, and the sound of the hoofs, and the sound of Keawe singing to himself for pleasure, echoed in the caverns of the dead. He came to the Bright House, and still he was singing. He sat and ate in the broad balcony, and the Chinaman wondered at his master, to hear how he sang between the mouthfuls. The sun went down into the sea, and the night came; and Keawe walked the balconies by lamplight, high on the mountains, and the voice of his singing startled men on ships.

"Here am I now upon my high place," he said to himself. "Life may be no better; this is the mountain top: and all shelves about me toward the worse. For the first time I will light up the chambers, and bathe in my fine bath with the hot water and the cold, and sleep alone in the bed of my bridal chamber."

So the Chinaman had word, and he must rise from sleep and light the furnaces; and as he wrought below, beside the boilers, he heard his master singing and rejoicing above him in the lighted chambers. When the water began to be hot the Chinaman cried to his master; and Keawe went into the bathroom; and the Chinaman heard him sing as he filled the marble basin; and heard him sing, and the singing broken, as he un-

dressed; until of a sudden the song ceased. The Chinaman listened, and listened; he called up the house to
Keawe to ask if all were well, and Keawe answered
him "Yes", and bade him go to bed; but there was no
more singing in the Bright House; and all night long
the Chinaman heard his master's feet go round and
round the balconies without repose.

Now the truth of it was this: as Keawe undressed for
his bath, he spied upon his flesh a patch like a patch of
lichen on a rock, and it was then that he stopped singing. For he knew the likeness of that patch, and knew
that he was fallen in the Chinese Evil—leprosy.

Now, it is a sad thing for any man to fall into this
sickness. And it would be a sad thing for anyone to
leave a house so beautiful and so commodious, and
depart from all his friends to the north coast of Molokai between the mighty cliff and the sea-breakers. But
what was that to the case of the man Keawe, he who
had met his love but yesterday, and won her but that
morning, and now saw all his hopes break, in a moment,
like a piece of glass?

A while he sat upon the edge of the bath; then
sprang, with a cry, and ran outside; and to and fro, to
and fro, along the balcony, like one despairing.

"Very willingly could I leave Hawaii, the home of
my fathers," Keawe was thinking. "Very lightly could
I leave my house, the high-placed, the many-windowed,
here upon the mountains. Very bravely could I go to
Molokai, to Kalaupapa by the cliffs, to live with the

smitten and to sleep there, far from my fathers. But what wrong have I done, what sin lies upon my soul, that I should have encountered Kokua coming from the sea-water in the evening? Kokua, the soul ensnarer! Kokua, the light of my life! Her may I never wed, her may I look upon no longer, her may I no more handle with my loving hand; and it is for this, it is for you, O Kokua! that I pour my lamentations!"

Now you are to observe what sort of a man Keawe was, for he might have dwelt there in the Bright House for years, and no one been the wiser of his sickness; but he reckoned nothing of that, if he must lose Kokua. And again, he might have wed Kokua even as he was; and so many would have done, because they have the souls of pigs; but Keawe loved the maid manfully, and he would do her no hurt and bring her in no danger.

A little beyond the midst of the night, there came in his mind the recollection of that bottle. He went round to the back porch, and called to memory the day when the devil had looked forth; and at the thought ice ran in his veins.

"A dreadful thing is the bottle," thought Keawe, "and dreadful is the imp, and it is a dreadful thing to risk the flames of hell. But what other hope have I to cure my sickness or to wed Kokua? What!" he thought, "would I beard the devil once, only to get me a house, and not face him again to win Kokua?"

Thereupon he called to mind it was the next day the *Hall* went by on her return to Honolulu. "There must

I go first," he thought, "and see Lopaka. For the best hope that I have now is to find that same bottle I was so pleased to be rid of."

Never a wink could he sleep, the food stuck in his throat; but he sent a letter to Kiano, and, about the time when the steamer would be coming, rode down beside the cliff of the tombs. It rained; his horse went heavily; he looked up at the black mouths of the caves, and he envied the dead that slept there and were done with trouble; and called to mind how he had galloped by the day before, and was astonished. So he came down to Hookena, and there was all the country gathered for the steamer as usual. In the shed before the store they sat and jested and passed the news; but there was no matter of speech in Keawe's bosom, and he sat in their midst and looked without on the rain falling on the houses, and the surf beating among the rocks, and the sighs arose in his throat.

"Keawe of the Bright House is out of spirits," said one to another. Indeed, and so he was, and little wonder.

Then the *Hall* came, and the whale-boat carried him on board. The after-part of the ship was full of Haoles — white people — who had been to visit the volcano as their custom is; and the midst was crowded with Kanakas, and the fore-part with wild bulls from Hilo and horses from Kaü; but Keawe sat apart from all in his sorrow and watched for the house of Kiano. There it sat, low upon the shore in the black rocks, and shaded by the cocoa-palms, and there by the door was a red holoku, no greater than a fly, and going to and fro with a fly's busyness. "Ah, queen of my heart," he cried, "I'll venture my dear soul to win you!"

Soon after, darkness fell, and the cabins were lit up, and the Haoles sat and played at the cards and drank whisky as their custom is; but Keawe walked the deck all night; and all the next day, as they steamed under the lee of Maui or of Molokai, he was still pacing to and fro like a wild animal in a menagerie.

Towards evening they passed Diamond Head, and came to the pier of Honolulu. Keawe stepped out and among the crowd and began to ask for Lopaka. It seemed he had become the owner of a schooner—none better in the islands—and was gone upon an adventure as far as Pola-Pola or Kahiki; so there was no help to be looked for from Lopaka. Keawe called to mind a friend of his, a lawyer in the town (I must not tell his name), and inquired of him. They said he was grown suddenly rich, and had a fine new house upon Waikiki shore; and this put a thought in Keawe's head, and he called a hack and drove to the lawyer's house.

The house was all brand new, and the trees in the garden no greater than walking-sticks, and the lawyer, when he came, had the air of a man well pleased.

"What can I do to serve you?" said the lawyer.

"You are a friend of Lopaka's," replied Keawe, "and Lopaka purchased from me a certain piece of goods that I thought you might enable me to trace."

The lawyer's face became very dark. "I do not profess to misunderstand you, Mr. Keawe," said he, "though this is an ugly business to be stirring in. You may be sure I know nothing, but yet I have a guess, and if you would apply in a certain quarter I think you might have news."

And he named the name of a man, which, again, I had better not repeat. So it was for days, and Keawe went from one to another finding everywhere new clothes and carriages, and fine new houses, and men everywhere in great contentment, although, to be sure, when he hinted at his business, their faces would cloud over.

"No doubt I am upon the track," thought Keawe. "These new clothes and carriages are all the gifts of the little imp, and these glad faces are the faces of men who have taken their profit and got rid of the accursed thing in safety. When I see pale cheeks and hear sighing, I shall know that I am near the bottle."

So it befell at last that he was recommended to a Haole in Beritania Street. When he came to the door, about the hour of the evening meal, there were the usual marks of the new house, and the young garden, and the electric light shining in the windows; but when the owner came, a shock of hope and fear ran through Keawe; for here was a young man, white as a corpse, and black about the eyes, the hair shedding from his head, and such a look in his countenance as a man may have when he is waiting for the gallows.

"Here it is, to be sure," thought Keawe, and so with

this man he noways veiled his errand. "I am come to buy the bottle," said he.

At his word, the young Haole of Beritania Street reeled against the wall.

"The bottle!" he gasped. "To buy the bottle!" Then he seemed to choke, and seizing Keawe by the arm carried him into a room and poured out wine in two glasses.

"Here is my respects," said Keawe, who had been much about with Haoles in his time. "Yes," he added, "I am come to buy the bottle. What is the price by now?"

At that word the young man let his glass slip through his fingers, and looked upon Keawe like a ghost.

"The price," says he; "the price! You do not know the price?"

"It is for that I am asking you," returned Keawe. "But why are you so much concerned? Is there anything wrong about the price?"

"It has dropped a great deal in value since your time, Mr. Keawe," said the young man, stammering.

"Well, well, I shall have the less to pay for it," says Keawe. "How much did it cost you?"

The young man was as white as a sheet. "Two cents," said he.

"What!" cried Keawe, "two cents? Why, then, you can only sell it for one. And he who buys it——" The words died upon Keawe's tongue; he who bought it could never sell it again, the bottle and the bottle imp must abide with him until he died, and when he died must carry him to the red end of hell.

The young man of Beritania Street fell upon his knees. "For God's sake, buy it!" he cried. "You can have all my fortune in the bargain. I was mad when I bought it at that price. I had embezzled money at my store; I was lost else: I must have gone to gaol."

"Poor creature," said Keawe, "you would risk your soul upon so desperate an adventure, and to avoid the proper punishment of your own disgrace; and you think I could hesitate with love in front of me. Give me the bottle, and the change which I make sure you have all ready. Here is a five-cent piece."

It was as Keawe supposed; the young man had the change ready in a drawer; the bottle changed hands, and Keawe's fingers were no sooner clasped upon the stalk than he had breathed his wish to be a clean man. And, sure enough, when he got home to his room, and stripped himself before a glass, his flesh was whole like an infant's. And here was the strange thing: he had no sooner seen the miracle than his mind was changed within him, and he cared naught for the Chinese Evil, and little enough for Kokua; and had but the one thought, that here he was bound to the bottle imp for time and for eternity, and had no better hope but to be a cinder for ever in the flames of hell. Away ahead of him he saw them blaze with his mind's eye, and his soul shrank, and darkness fell upon the light.

When Keawe came to himself a little, he was aware

it was the night when the band played at the hotel. Thither he went, because he feared to be alone; and there, among happy faces, walked to and fro, and heard the tunes go up and down, and saw Berger beat the measure, and all the while he heard the flames crackle, and saw the red fire burning in the bottomless pit. Of a sudden the band played *Hiki-ao-ao*; that was a song that he had sung with Kokua, and at the strain courage returned to him.

"It is done now," he thought, "and once more let me take the good along with the evil."

So it befell that he returned to Hawaii by the first steamer, and as soon as it could be managed he was wedded to Kokua, and carried her up the mountainside to the Bright House.

Now it was so with these two, that when they were together, Kaewe's heart was stilled; but so soon as he was alone he fell into a brooding horror, and heard the flames crackle, and saw the red fire burn in the bottomless pit. The girl, indeed, had come to him wholly; her heart leapt in her side at sight of him, her hand clung to his; and she was so fashioned from the hair upon her head to the nails upon her toes that none could see her without joy. She was pleasant in her nature. She had the good word always. Full of song she was, and went to and fro in the Bright House, the brightest thing in its three storeys, carolling like the birds. And Keawe beheld and heard her with delight, and then must shrink upon one side, and weep and groan to think upon the price that he had paid for her; and then he must dry his eyes, and wash his face, and go and sit with her on the broad balconies, joining in her songs, and, with a sick spirit, answering her smiles.

There came a day when her feet began to be heavy and her songs more rare; and now it was not Keawe only that would weep apart, but each would sunder from the other and sit in opposite balconies with the whole width of the Bright House betwixt. Keawe was so sunk in his despair he scarce observed the change, and was only glad he had more hours to sit alone and brood upon his destiny, and was not so frequently condemned to pull a smiling face on a sick heart. But one day, coming softly through the house, he heard the sound of a child sobbing, and there was Kokua rolling her face upon the balcony floor, and weeping like the lost.

"You do well to weep in this house, Kokua," he said. "And yet I would give the head off my body that you (at least) might have been happy."

"Happy!" she cried. "Keawe, when you lived alone in your Bright House, you were the word of the island for a happy man; laughter and song were in your mouth, and your face was as bright as the sunrise. Then you wedded poor Kokua; and the good God knows what is amiss in her—but from that day you have not smiled. O!" she cried, "what ails me? I thought I was pretty, and I knew I loved him. What ails me that I throw this cloud upon my husband?"

"Poor Kokua," said Keawe. He sat down by her side, and sought to take her hand; but that she plucked away. "Poor Kokua!" he said again. "My poor child—my pretty. And I had thought all this while to spare you! Well, you shall know all. Then, at least, you will pity poor Keawe; then you will understand how much he loved you in the past—that he dared hell for your possession—and how much he loves you still (the poor condemned one), that he can yet call up a smile when he beholds you."

With that he told her all, even from the beginning.

"You have done this for me?" she cried. "Ah, well, then what do I care!"—and she clasped and wept upon him.

"Ah, child!" said Keawe, "and yet, when I consider of the fire of hell, I care a good deal!"

"Never tell me," said she; "no man can be lost because he loved Kokua, and no other fault. I tell you, Keawe, I shall save you with these hands, or perish in your company. What! you loved me, and gave your soul, and you think I will not die to save you in return?"

"Ah, my dear! you might die a hundred times, and what difference would that make?" he cried, "except to leave me lonely till the time comes of my damnation?"

"You know nothing," said she. "I was educated in a school in Honolulu; I am no common girl. And I tell you, I shall save my lover. What is this you say about a cent? But all the world is not American. In England

they have a piece they call a farthing, which is about half a cent. Ah! sorrow!" she cried, "that makes it scarcely better, for the buyer must be lost, and we shall find none so brave as my Keawe! But then, there is France: they have a small coin there which they call a centime, and these go five to the cent, or thereabout. We could not do better. Come, Keawe, let us go to the French islands; let us go to Tahiti as fast as ships can bear us. There we have four centimes, three centimes, two centimes, one centime; four possible sales to come and go on; and two of us to push the bargain. Come, my Keawe! kiss me, and banish care. Kokua will defend you."

"Gift of God!" he cried. "I cannot think that God will punish me for desiring aught so good! Be it as you will, then; take me where you please: I put my life and my salvation in your hands."

Early the next day Kokua was about her preparations. She took Keawe's chest that he went with sailoring; and first she put the bottle in a corner; and then packed it with the richest of their clothes and the bravest of the knick-knacks in the house. "For," said she, "we must seem to be rich folks, or who will believe in the bottle?" All the time of her preparation she was as gay as a bird; only when she looked upon Keawe the tears would spring in her eye, and she must run and kiss him. As for Keawe, a weight was off his soul; now that he had his secret shared, and some hope in front of him, he seemed like a new man, his feet went lightly on the earth, and his breath was good to him again. Yet was terror still at his elbow; and ever and again, as the wind blows out a taper, hope died in him, and he saw the flames toss and the red fire burn in hell.

It was given out in the country they were gone pleasuring to the States, which was thought a strange thing, and yet not so strange as the truth, if any could have guessed it. So they went to Honolulu in the *Hall*, and thence in the *Umatilla* to San Francisco with a crowd of Haoles, and at San Francisco took their passage by the mail brigantine, the *Tropic Bird*, for Papeete, the chief place of the French in the south islands. Thither they came, after a pleasant voyage, on a fair day of the trade wind, and saw the reef with the surf breaking, and Motuiti with its palms, and the schooner riding withinside, and the white houses of the town low down along the shore among green trees, and overhead the mountains and the clouds of Tahiti, the wise island.

It was judged the most wise to hire a house, which they did accordingly, opposite the British Consul's, to make a great parade of money, and themselves conspicuous with carriages and horses. This it was very easy to do, so long as they had the bottle in their possession; for Kokua was more bold than Keawe, and, whenever she had a mind, called on the imp for twenty or a hundred dollars. At this rate they soon grew to be remarked in the town; and the strangers from Hawaii, their riding and their driving, the fine holokus and the rich lace of Kokua, became the matter of much talk.

They got on well after the first with the Tahitian language, which is indeed like to the Hawaiian, with a change of certain letters: and as soon as they had any freedom of speech, began to push the bottle. You are to consider it was not an easy subject to introduce; it was not easy to persuade people you were in earnest, when you offered to sell them for four centimes the spring of health and riches inexhaustible. It was necessary besides to explain the dangers of the bottle; and either people disbelieved the whole thing and laughed, or they thought the more of the darker part, became overcast with gravity, and drew away from Keawe and Kokua, as from persons who had dealings with the devil. So far from gaining ground, these two began to find they were avoided in the town; the children ran away from them screaming, a thing intolerable to Kokua; Catholics crossed themselves as they went by; and all persons began with one accord to disengage themselves from their advances.

Depression fell upon their spirits. They would sit at night in their new house, after a day's weariness, and not exchange one word, or the silence would be broken by Kokua bursting suddenly into sobs. Sometimes they would pray together; sometimes they would have the bottle out upon the floor, and sit all evening watching how the shadow hovered in the midst. At such times they would be afraid to go to rest. It was long ere slumber came to them, and, if either dozed off, it would be to wake and find the other silently weeping in the dark, or, perhaps, to wake alone, the other having fled from the house and the neighbourhood of that bottle, to pace under the bananas in the little garden, or to wander on the beach by moonlight.

One night it was so when Kokua awoke. Keawe was gone. She felt in the bed, and his place was cold. Then fear fell upon her, and she sat up in bed. A little moonshine filtered through the shutters. The room was bright, and she could spy the bottle on the floor. Outside it blew high, the great trees of the avenue cried aloud, and the fallen leaves rattled in the verandah. In the midst of this Kokua was aware of another sound; whether of a beast or of a man she could scarce tell, but it was as sad as death, and cut her to the soul. Softly she arose, set the door ajar, and looked forth into the moonlit yard. There, under the bananas, lay Keawe, his mouth in the dust, and as he lay he moaned.

It was Kokua's first thought to run forward and console him; her second potently withheld her. Keawe had borne himself before his wife like a brave man; it became her little in the hour of weakness to intrude upon his shame. With the thought she drew back into the house.

"Heaven!" she thought, "how careless have I been— how weak! It is he, not I, that stands in this eternal peril; it was he, not I, that took the curse upon his soul. It is for my sake, and for the love of a creature of so little worth and such poor help, that he now beholds so close to him the flames of hell—ay, and smells the smoke of it, lying without there in the wind and moonlight. Am I so dull of spirit that never till now I have surmised my duty, or have I seen it before and turned aside? But now, at least, I take up my soul in both the hands of my affection; now I say farewell to the white steps of heaven and the waiting faces of my friends. A love for a love, and let mine be equalled with Keawe's! A soul for a soul, and be it mine to perish!"

She was a deft woman with her hands, and was soon apparelled. She took in her hands the change—the precious centimes they kept ever at their side; for this coin is little used, and they had made provision at a government office. When she was forth in the avenue clouds came upon the wind, and the moon was blackened. The town slept, and she knew not whither to turn till she heard one coughing in the shadow of the trees.

"Old man," said Kokua, "what do you here abroad in the cold night?"

The old man could scarce express himself for coughing, but she made out that he was old and poor, and a stranger in the island.

"Will you do me a service?" said Kokua. "As one stranger to another, and as an old man to a young woman, will you help a daughter of Hawaii?"

"Ah," said the old man. "So you are the witch from the Eight Islands, and even my old soul you seek to entangle. But I have heard of you, and defy your wickedness."

"Sit down here," said Kokua, "and let me tell you a tale." And she told him the story of Keawe from the beginning to the end.

"And now," said she, "I am his wife, whom he bought with his soul's welfare. And what should I do? If I went to him myself and offered to buy it, he would refuse. But if you go, he will sell it eagerly; I will await you here; you will buy it for four centimes, and I will buy it again for three. And the Lord strengthen a poor girl!"

"If you meant falsely," said the old man, "I think God would strike you dead."

"He would!" cried Kokua. "Be sure He would. I could not be so treacherous—God would not suffer it."

"Give me the four centimes and await me here," said the old man.

Now, when Kokua stood alone in the street her spirit died. The wind roared in the trees, and it seemed to her the rushing of the flames of hell; the shadows tossed in the light of the street lamp, and they seemed to her the snatching hands of evil ones. If she had had the strength, she must have run away, and if she had had the breath she must have screamed aloud; but in truth she could do neither, and stood and trembled in the avenue, like an affrighted child.

Then she saw the old man returning, and he had the bottle in his hand.

"I have done your bidding," said he. "I left your husband weeping like a child; tonight he will sleep easy." And he held the bottle forth.

"Before you give it to me," Kokua panted, "take the good with the evil—ask to be delivered from your cough."

"I am an old man," replied the other, "and too near the gate of the grave to take a favour from the devil. But what is this? Why do you not take the bottle? Do you hesitate?"

"Not hesitate," cried Kokua. "I am only weak. Give me a moment. It is my hand resists, my flesh shrinks back from the accursed thing. One moment only!"

The old man looked upon Kokua kindly. "Poor child!" said he, "you fear; your soul misgives you. Well, let me keep it. I am old, and can never more be happy in this world, and as for the next—"

"Give it to me!" gasped Kokua. "There is your money. Do you think I am so base as that? Give me the bottle."

"God bless you, child," said the old man.

Kokua concealed the bottle under her holoku, said farewell to the old man, and walked off along the avenue, she cared not whither. For all roads were now the same to her, and led equally to hell. Sometimes she walked, and sometimes ran; sometimes she screamed out loud in the night, and sometimes lay by the wayside in the dust and wept. All that she had heard of hell came back to her; she saw the flames blaze, and she smelt the smoke, and her flesh withered on the coals.

Near day she came to her mind again, and returned to the house. It was even as the old man said—Keawe slumbered like a child. Kokua stood and gazed upon his face.

"Now, my husband," said she, "it is your turn to sleep. When you wake it will be your turn to sing and laugh. But for poor Kokua, alas! that meant no evil— for poor Kokua no more sleep, no more singing, no more delight, whether in earth or heaven."

With that she lay down in the bed by his side, and her misery was so extreme that she fell in a deep slumber instantly.

Later in the morning her husband woke and gave her the good news. It seemed he was silly with delight, for he paid no heed to her distress, ill though she dissembled it. The words stuck in her mouth, it mattered not; Keawe did the speaking. She ate not a bite, but who was to observe it? for Keawe cleared the dish. Kokua saw and heard him, like some strange thing in a dream; there were times when she forgot or doubted, and put her hands to her brow; to know herself doomed and hear her husband babble seemed so monstrous.

All the while Keawe was eating and talking, and planning the time of their return, and thanking her for saving him, and fondling her, and calling her the true helper after all. He laughed at the old man that was fool enough to buy that bottle.

"A worthy old man he seemed," Keawe said. "But

no one can judge by appearances. For why did the old reprobate require the bottle?"

"My husband," said Kokua humbly, "his purpose may have been good."

Keawe laughed like an angry man.

"Fiddle-de-dee!" cried Keawe. "An old rogue, I tell you, and an old ass to boot. For the bottle was hard enough to sell at four centimes; and at three it will be quite impossible. The margin is not broad enough, the thing begins to smell of scorching—brrr!" said he, and shuddered. "It is true I bought it myself at a cent, when I knew not there were smaller coins. I was a fool for my pains; there will never be found another: and whoever has that bottle now will carry it to the pit."

"O my husband!" said Kokua. "Is it not a terrible thing to save oneself by the eternal ruin of another? It seems to me I could not laugh. I would be humbled. I would be filled with melancholy. I would pray for the poor holder."

Then Keawe, because he felt the truth of what she said, grew the more angry. "Heighty-teighty!" cried he, "you may be filled with melancholy if you please. It is not the mind of a good wife. If you thought at all of me you would sit shamed."

Thereupon he went out, and Kokua was alone.

What chance had she to sell that bottle at two centimes? None, she perceived. And if she had any, here was her husband hurrying her away to a country where there was nothing lower than a cent. And here—on the morrow of her sacrifice—was her husband leaving her and blaming her.

She would not even try to profit by what time she had, but sat in the house, and now had the bottle out and viewed it with unutterable fear, and now, with loathing, hid it out of sight.

By and by Keawe came back, and would have her take a drive.

"My husband, I am ill," she said, "I am out of heart. Excuse me, I can take no pleasure."

Then was Keawe more wroth than ever. With her, because he thought she was brooding over the case of the old man; and with himself, because he thought she was right, and was ashamed to be so happy.

"This is your truth," cried he, "and this your affection! Your husband is just saved from eternal ruin, which he encountered for the love of you—and you can take no pleasure! Kokua, you have a disloyal heart."

He went forth again furious, and wandered in the town all day. He met friends, and drank with them; they hired a carriage and drove into the country, and there drank again. All the time Keawe was ill at ease, because he was taking this pastime while his wife was sad, and because he knew in his heart that she was more right than he; and the knowledge made him drink the deeper.

Now there was an old brutal Haole drinking with him, one that had been a boatswain of a whaler, a runaway, a digger in gold mines, a convict in prisons.

He had a low mind and a foul mouth; he loved to drink and to see others drunken; and he pressed the glass upon Keawe. Soon there was no more money in the company.

"Here, you!" said the boatswain, "you are rich, you have always been saying. You have a bottle or some foolishness."

"Yes," says Keawe, "I am rich; I will go back and get some money from my wife, who keeps it."

"That's a bad idea, mate," said the boatswain. "Never you trust a petticoat with dollars. They're all as false as water; you keep an eye on her."

Now this word stuck in Keawe's mind; for he was muddled with what he had been drinking.

"I should not wonder but she was false, indeed," thought he. "Why else should she be so cast down at my release? But I will show her I am not the man to be fooled. I will catch her in the act."

Accordingly, when they were back in town, Keawe bade the boatswain wait for him at the corner, by the old calaboose, and went forward up the avenue alone to the door of his house. The night had come again; there was a light within, but never a sound; and Keawe crept about the corner, opened the back-door softly, and looked in.

There was Kokua on the floor, the lamp at her side; before her was a milk-white bottle, with a round belly and a long neck; and as she viewed it, Kokua wrung her hands.

A long time Keawe stood and looked in the doorway. At first he was struck stupid; and then fear fell upon him that the bargain had been made amiss, and the bottle had come back to him as it came at San Francisco; and at that his knees were loosened, and the fumes of the wine departed from his head like mists off a river in the morning. And then he had another thought; and it was a strange one, that made his cheeks to burn.

"I must make sure of this," thought he.

So he closed the door, and went softly round the corner again, and then came noisily in, as though he were but now returned. And, lo! by the time he opened the front door no bottle was to be seen; and Kokua sat in a chair and started up like one awakened out of sleep.

"I have been drinking all day and making merry," said Keawe. "I have been with good companions, and now I only come back for money, and return to drink and carouse with them again."

Both his face and voice were as stern as judgement, but Kokua was too troubled to observe.

"You do well to use your own, my husband," said she, and her words trembled.

"O, I do well in all things," said Keawe, and he went straight to the chest and took out money. But he looked besides in the corner where they kept the bottle, and there was no bottle there.

At that the chest heaved upon the floor like a sea-billow, and the house span about him like a wreath of smoke, for he saw he was lost now, and there was no escape. "It is what I feared," he thought. "It is she who has bought it."

And then he came to himself a little and rose up; but the sweat streamed on his face as thick as the rain and as cold as the well-water.

"Kokua," said he, "I said to you today what ill became me. Now I return to carouse with my jolly companions," and at that he laughed a little quietly. "I will take more pleasure in the cup if you forgive me."

She clasped his knees in a moment; she kissed his knees with flowing tears.

"O," she cried, "I asked but a kind word!"

"Let us never one think hardly of the other," said Keawe, and was gone out of the house.

Now, the money that Keawe had taken was only some of that store of centime pieces they had laid in at their arrival. It was very sure he had no mind to be drinking. His wife had given her soul for him, now he must give his for hers; no other thought was in the world with him.

At the corner, by the old calaboose, there was the boatswain waiting.

"My wife has the bottle," said Keawe, "and, unless you help me to recover it, there can be no more money and no more liquor tonight."

"You do not mean to say you are serious about that bottle?" cried the boatswain.

"There is the lamp," said Keawe. "Do I look as if I was jesting?"

"That is so," said the boatswain. "You look as serious as a ghost."

"Well, then," said Keawe, "here are two centimes; you must go to my wife in the house, and offer her these for the bottle, which (if I am not much mistaken) she will give you instantly. Bring it to me here, and I will buy it back from you for one; for that is the law with this bottle, that it still must be sold for a less sum. But whatever you do, never breathe a word to her that you have come from me."

"Mate, I wonder are you making a fool of me?" asked the boatswain.

"It will do you no harm if I am," returned Keawe.

"That is so, mate," said the boatswain.

"And if you doubt me," added Keawe, "you can try. As soon as you are clear of the house, wish to have your pocket full of money, or a bottle of the best rum, or what you please, and you will see the virtue of the thing."

"Very well, Kanaka," says the boatswain. "I will try; but if you are having your fun out of me, I will take my fun out of you with a belaying-pin."

So the whaler-man went off up the avenue; and Keawe stood and waited. It was near the same spot where Kokua had waited the night before; but Keawe was more resolved, and never faltered in his purpose; only his soul was bitter with despair.

It seemed a long time he had to wait before he heard a voice singing in the darkness of the avenue. He knew the voice to be the boatswain's; but it was strange how drunken it appeared upon a sudden.

Next, the man himself came stumbling into the light of the lamp. He had the devil's bottle buttoned in his coat; another bottle was in his hand; and even as he came in view he raised it to his mouth and drank.

"You have it," said Keawe. "I see that."

"Hands off!" cried the boatswain, jumping back. "Take a step near me and I'll smash your mouth. You thought you could make a cat's-paw of me, did you?"

"What do you mean?" cried Keawe.

"Mean?" cried the boatswain. "This is a pretty good bottle, this is; that's what I mean. How I got it for two centimes I can't make out; but I'm sure you shan't have it for one."

"You mean you won't sell it?" gasped Keawe.

"No, *sir*!" cried the boatswain. "But I'll give you a drink of the rum, if you like."

"I tell you," said Keawe, "the man who has that bottle goes to hell."

"I reckon I'm going anyway," returned the sailor; "and this bottle's the best thing to go with I've struck yet. No, sir!" he cried again, "this is my bottle now, and you can go and fish for another."

"Can this be true?" Keawe cried. "For your own sake, I beseech you, sell it me!"

"I don't value any of your talk," replied the boatswain. "You thought I was a flat; now you see I'm not; and there's an end. If you won't have a swallow of the rum I'll have one myself. Here's your health, and good-night to you!"

So off he went down the avenue towards town, and there goes the bottle out of the story.

But Keawe ran to Kokua light as the wind; and great was their joy that night; and great, since then, has been the peace of all their days in the Bright House.

# THE BOOTS THAT NEVER WORE OUT

## DOROTHY GLADYS SPICER

*In which young Jussi outwits the Devil in a series of clever confrontations and wins for himself a pair of boots soled with Devil's hide. To this day men of Suomi (Finland) talk of the boots that never wore out, and kept Finland free of devils forever.*

ONCE ON a time, a Devil told his wife they'd leave Hell for a while and visit Suomi, or Finland, a land of birch and pine forests and a thousand sparkling lakes and, as the Devils had to admit, a land of men who gave trouble. It was impossible to get the better of them and lure them to Hell for their own destruction.

"In Suomi, we'll get a farm, and take our own animals with us. I'll bargain with a man, fray his temper. And then," gloated the Evil One, his eyes round and bright, "he'll have to bargain with me! Then he will be mine and I'll drag him down to Hell."

Now while the Devil was scheming in Hell, the young Jussi, on earth, was working hard enough for three. His two elder brothers, wearied of the dull life on their father's poor farm, had gone adventuring, one day. And once away, they never returned. Three years had

58

passed, and still no word was heard from them.

But absence makes the heart fonder, so goes the old saying. And the longer they stayed away, the more lustily did the parents praise their remarkable sons.

"Our boys have gone into the world to seek fortune and fame," the aged couple boasted. "They'll come back, never fear. And when they do, they'll dress us like rich folks, and feed us fancy cakes and wine."

When people reminded the doting oldsters that meanwhile their youngest son, Jussi, was doing his brothers' work, as well as his own, his father shrugged.

"Jussi, ah yes," he said with scorn. "He's content to plough and sow, milk cows and feed pigs. He's not one for adventuring and making a fortune."

"As if I wouldn't like to," sighed Jussi. "But with my brothers gone—and our parents so old—my place is here." Then he went to the barn whistling. For Jussi loved his parents dearly, despite their harsh words.

But one night, he had a change of heart. After he'd gone to bed and the old people fancied him asleep, Jussi heard his father say:

"Our youngest son isn't like the others. He'll never amount to a hill of beans. All he'll ever do is potter."

"Alas, yes," the youth's mother agreed. "He's not clever enough to seek his fortune or care for us when we can't work."

"Ah, well, he who eavesdrops hears no good of himself," Jussi said sadly. "I'll go away this very night. But I'll be back, come harvest," he added hastily, con-

vinced that his brothers never would return. When his
parents were asleep, he threw on his clothes and crept
to the door. It would do them good to fend for themselves for a time, he decided.

Outside, the air was crisp, the stars close. "I could
pick you like buttercups," Jussi cried joyfully and
reached up his arms. Tingling with excitement, he
pelted towards the crossroads. He was free—his own
man. At last he, too, was going adventuring. "I'll head
south, where I'll find farms to work on for food—till I
can make my fortune."

The rest of the night and all next day, Jussi slogged
along the road. But he saw no farms. As dusk closed in,
he was dismayed. His feet were like stones, his stomach
a yawning sack. Just as he thought he'd best curl up
beside the road, the lad saw a light. "Ho, a farm's
yonder," he cried, and quickened his step.

It was then Jussi heard a voice, from somewhere
behind, say, "If it's work you want, I'm looking for a
husky lad. And I offer good bed and board."

Jussi turned quickly and saw a dark figure step out
from the shadows.

"Oh!" he gasped. "But you're—you're—" He stopped
in fright and in confusion. For the stranger's eyes
glowed in the fast-fading light. He had horns and
cloven feet and a long twitching tail.

"I'm a Devil, yes," the stranger admitted, chuckling.
"But don't be afraid. I'm master here. My wife and I
live in the house beyond the hedge. She's fixing soup

and stew now, and from the looks of you, you could do with both. Will you come home to supper with us?" he asked kindly.

At mention of soup and stew, Jussi drooled. At the same time, his skin prickled. Yet he'd wanted adventure, and here it was.

"Thank you," he said. "I do need food, and I'd like to work for you."

"I was sure you would," the Devil said easily. "Work starts at dawn. But tonight we'll celebrate our bargain."

Jussi pricked up his ears, though by now he was so tired he knew he would agree to anything. "A bargain, eh?" he asked.

"Oh, nothing, really," the Devil assured him, waving his tail airily. "Whichever one loses his temper first shall owe the other a patch of hide from his back, a patch big enough to sole a pair of shoes. Besides, I'll expect you to do every task I set you—unless you want to give up your soul," he added.

"Well, all right," Jussi agreed, promising himself he'd not be the one to forfeit his skin—and he'd hold on to his soul, too. He was so hungry now, he'd die if he didn't eat soon.

The Devil was already leading the way to the lighted window. When they'd passed the hedge and turned in at the gate, there was the door. As the Master lifted the latch and pushed it open, Jussi found himself inside a cosy kitchen. And when he sniffed the appetizing aroma from the bubbling pot, he wasn't sorry he'd decided to serve the Devil.

Seeing her husband enter with the lad, the Mistress, who was grizzled and grey, stepped forward to welcome him. She seated Jussi at the white scrubbed table and dished out the soup. When she placed the brimming bowl before him, he thought he'd done well by himself.

After the youth had eaten all he could hold, and his head wobbled drowsily, the Master said briskly, "You'll sleep in the shed, next to the kitchen. But first, we'll seal our bargain with honey mead."

Having drunk the mead, Jussi was sleepier than ever. But when he finally stretched out on his cot and pulled up the covers, he mumbled contentedly, "Devil or not, he's not so bad. But he'll not get my hide—" In less than a minute the youth was sleeping soundly.

He was up before dawn, and after a hearty breakfast the Devil pointed to a pile of empty grain sacks. "Carry them to the barn," he ordered. "Before supper, I'll expect you to have them filled with grain and piled on the floor, ready to cart to the mill."

"Yes, Master," Jussi said. Shouldering the sacks, he went off whistling to his task.

But after he'd worked awhile, Jussi discovered something strange. No sooner were the sacks filled and securely tied than the grain trickled away through a mysterious hole at the bottom. After the same thing happened several times, he was convinced this was the Devil's bewitchment. "If the Master thinks I'll lose

my temper over *this*, he has another think coming!''
the lad said and sat down on a heavy upturned measure,
to decide what to do next.

Suddenly, a horrible yowling from under the sacks
made Jussi leap to his feet. ''Ha,'' he exclaimed. ''So
the Devil's cat is clawing holes in the sacks!'' Soon
grain and sacks were flying as he tore the pile apart.
And sure enough, at the bottom, two baleful eyes
peered into his.

Before Jussi could grab at the creature, however, she
flew at him, snarling. She sank vicious claws into his
arm. Faint with pain, he groped out blindly towards
the measure. How he managed to lift it, once his fingers
closed on the rim, he never knew. But after he'd
smashed the thing down on the demon cat's head, she
lay limp as an ugly black rag. ''Good riddance to you!''
grunted the youth. ''I'll wager no grain will spill now!''

And it didn't. At last, Jussi was able to fill the sacks.
He stacked them, fat and bulging with grain, on the
floor of the barn, and then went to supper.

''I must say, Mistress, I never tasted better soup,''
Jussi told the Devil's wife when she'd filled his bowl
three times.

All the while, the Devil stared suspiciously. ''I see
you have a good appetite, Jussi,'' he remarked. ''Did
you fill all the sacks with grain?''

''Oh, yes, Master, I did,'' Jussi replied, scraping his
bowl.

''Did you—did you see anything?'' the Devil asked.

"Only a horrid black cat, Master," said Jussi. "But I smashed her head."

"You WHAT?" bawled the Devil. "You killed my cat?"

"Oh, was the nasty thing yours?" Jussi asked, biting into his goat cheese. "She almost clawed off my arm."

"And too bad she didn't," snarled the Devil, his eyes glittering.

"There, there, Master," Jussi soothed. "You'd not be losing your temper, surely, for a dead cat."

"No, I'd not, if that's what you want!" said the Devil, pressing his lips together. After all, the lad had done his task. The Master took his wife by the arm and stumped off to bed without saying good night.

In the morning, the Devil told Jussi to hitch the oxen and go to the forest for logs. "When it's time to come home, I'll send my dog to show the way. You're to follow the same route he takes," he added with a smug smile.

"You can count on it, Master," Jussi said. Swinging himself to the wagon seat, he creaked through the gate, and down the long road. But all the while, he was wondering what scheme the Devil had up his sleeve. "Ah well, we'll find out soon enough," he told the oxen as they plodded toward the woods.

All day, Jussi loaded logs on the wagon. He'd barely finished when he heard a snarl. Then the Devil's dog bounded toward him, baring his sharp long teeth.

"All right, we're ready," Jussi cried and snatched up the reins. "You lead. We'll follow wherever you go."

The dog streaked ahead, taking, at first, the same route Jussi and the oxen had travelled. But when he reached the gate, instead of turning in, the creature paused at a small hole in the hedge. He looked back, lolling his tongue. And then, with a howl so chilling it froze the blood in the lad's veins, the dog leaped through the opening. "Ah-ha—so that's the route we're to follow." Jussi sighed. "Everything is bewitched—yesterday the cat, now the dog."

Knowing the dreadful thing he must do, Jussi drove the oxen on till they reached the hedge. Then he cut them to pieces, which he poked through the hole. He pushed the logs through, one by one, and then the wagon, chopped to bits. Last of all, Jussi stretched himself lean and long as a pole. By turning this way and wriggling that, he finally worked his body through the hole in the hedge.

That night at supper, the Devil eyed Jussi sharply and then asked, "Did you do as I said—follow my dog where he led?"

"Yes, Master, I came the same way," mumbled Jussi, his mouth full of fish.

"You m-mean—" the Devil faltered, more disturbed than he cared to admit.

"That I did as you said," replied the lad, wiping his lips on his hand.

"Any fool would have known it was impossible to get

through the hole," the Devil said.

"I only followed your instructions, Master, and a bargain's a bargain," replied Jussi.

The Devil's tail quivered. "What did you do with my oxen, my cart?" he demanded.

"Oh, they're out there, Master, beside the hedge— though, of course, I had to cut them up," Jussi said. "You can see for yourself."

By now the Devil, white with rage, leaped forward. But the lad held up his hand. "Tut, tut, Master, take care," he mocked. "You'd not want to lose your temper, and also your hide, for a team of oxen and a cart!"

"No, blockhead, I'd not," blustered the Devil, sitting down suddenly. "Now get out of my sight," he growled, his eyes smouldering.

Yawning tremendously, Jussi went to his room, but not to sleep. For when he heard the Devil talking in low tones to his wife, the lad strained his ears to catch every word.

"You must kill the boy at once," the Devil's wife was saying. "All he does is plot our ruin, and eat. Besides, if you don't take care, you'll forget and—"

"Never fear," said the Devil with a laugh that made Jussi's flesh creep. "Call me at midnight. I'll lop off his head with my sword while he sleeps."

Jussi shook his head. "I'm not so sure, Master," he muttered and grinned broadly. For while the pair was scheming to kill him, he'd made plans, too.

By midnight, when the Devil's wife hissed, "Psst! It's time now," Jussi had everything ready. Inside the bed, where his body usually lay, he had placed an ironbound keg, and on the pillow a stone.

"What with only moonlight to see by, and covers tucked in all around, it will seem that I'm lying there," chuckled the youth. Then he settled under the bed and started to snore.

And none too soon, for the next instant the lad heard the light click of the Devil's hooves approaching the door. He pushed it open, inch by inch. And when he'd entered the room, he listened intently, then lifted his arm. Jussi snored louder. In the dim light he saw steel flash.

The sword whistled through the air and then, with a terrific WHAM, the Devil brought it down on the stone. Jussi stopped breathing in mid-snore. "What a hard head," the Master grunted, running a thumb along the edge of the sword. "So hard it's made a nick."

Just to be sure the lad was dead, the Devil struck again—this time with such force that sparks flew from the hidden stone. "I've fixed him now," he said. "But I'll take a whack lower down."

With this blow the sword hit the keg. And when it flew apart, with splintering of wood and bursting of iron, the Devil went back to his wife. "He was tough to kill," he said. "But now he's dead, and we're rid of the sly meddling fellow."

Jussi crawled up from under the bed. "Wait and see,

Master," he murmured drowsily. Then he cleared out his bed, and slept soundly the rest of the night.

Jussi rose at dawn, to fetch water and build up the fire. When his Devil and his wife beheld him alive and nimble at the hearth, they thought they were seeing a ghost. But the lad was real enough, and with not a scratch on him! "D-did you sleep well?" the Devil asked, unable to keep his teeth from chattering.

"Never better, Master, until midnight, that is," replied Jussi. "Then something dropped from the ceiling and hit my nose twice. And just as I was dozing off, a muscle cramped in my leg."

Shaking with terror, the Devil sent Jussi to the barn and turned to his wife. "We'll go to market at once," he said. "And I'll give him a task that—"

"That what?" snapped the old creature testily. "You said you'd killed him, and now—"

"Now I know steel can't harm him," the Devil said. "Tonight I'll try fire."

Then the Master told Jussi to hitch up the mare. And with his mind still on the fire he planned to use to destroy Jussi, the Devil said, "While we're at market, you're to make the house flaming red."

What he meant was for Jussi to paint the house red, and, of course, he knew this. But what the lad said was, "Flaming red—while you're gone. But that's impossible, Master." Yet, in spite of his pretended dismay, he was considering a daring plan—a plan that couldn't fail.

"Impossible or not, you'd better do it," growled the Devil.

"I'll do my best, Master," Jussi said, watching the Devil crack his whip and rattle from the gate.

When the pair disappeared around the bend in the road, Jussi slapped his thigh and laughed uproariously. "Flaming red, eh? It's not so impossible, Master, as I made out," he said, and went into another gale of laughter.

When he thought the Devil and his wife had reached market, Jussi lighted a brand and set fire to the house. As the flames licked up, the sky glowed three leagues around. "You'll be rushing back soon, Master," Jussi predicted. "And when you do—" he added, fingering the knife at his belt.

It wasn't long before the pounding of hooves on the road told Jussi he was right. "The Master's coming on the mare's back," he said, cocking an ear. "He's left the cart, and his wife, behind." Just then the Devil dashed around the bend, clutching at the mare's mane, prodding her flanks with the forked end of his tail.

Plunging headlong through the gate, the Devil sprang from the horse's back. "What do you mean— burning my house while I'm at market?" he roared.

"Why, Master, I thought you'd be pleased," Jussi said, with a hurt look. "You said, make the house flaming red, and I did. I thought I got a pretty colour."

"You—you knothead," bellowed the Devil. "You knew very well I meant for you to paint the house—

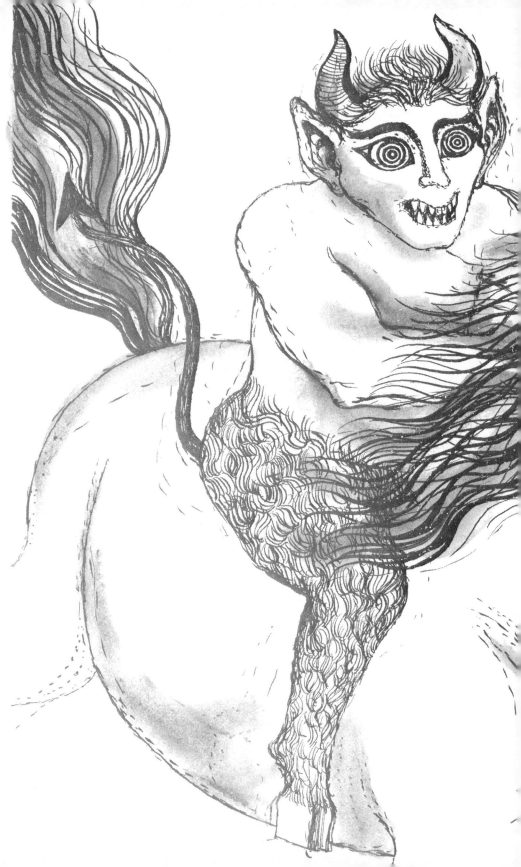

all of it." He reached horrible hands towards Jussi's throat. "Wait till I catch you. I'll drag you to Hell and burn you to a crisp."

"Careful, Master," Jussi warned pleasantly. "I've done my task. You're losing your temper, and all for a burning house."

"Yes, I am, and I'm glad!" shrieked the Devil, casting caution aside. "And if you don't wipe that smirk from your face and get out, I'll—I'll—"

"You'll what, Master?" Jussi taunted, for the Devil, beside himself with rage, now choked helplessly. "I'll get out when you've paid me what you owe me."

"Paid what I owe you," sputtered the Devil. "For killing my oxen, chopping up my wagon, burning my house? Pay you, indeed!"

Again the enraged fiend reached toward Jussi. But he caught him deftly by the tail and held him as in a vice. "A bargain's a bargain, Master, in case you've forgotten," the youth said. "You have lost your temper and you've admitted it. Now you must pay."

The demon stamped and bawled until the flaming house crashed to the ground. He whined and begged when he saw Jussi draw out his knife. But the lad paid no heed until he'd taken a generous patch of black swarthy hide from his Master's back. "Now that I have enough skin for a pair of soles—and also the tops—of a pair of boots, you'd best go," Jussi advised, releasing the Devil. "And if I ever see your ugly face around here again—"

With a loud yell, the Devil was off, howling all the way back to Hell—and behind him tagged his evil animals. "I'll have no dealing with Suomi folk ever again. The other devils were right," he admitted to his wife, later, when she joined him in the Underworld. "The men are hard to snare—tricky—and too stupid, even, to lose their tempers."

No sooner had the Devil disappeared than lo! a new farm, better by far, rose out of the smoking rubble. As Jussi gazed at the snug house and the fine barn, with pens for the pigs and coops for the chickens, he rejoiced exceedingly. "As soon as I get my boots made and soled with the Devil's hide, I'll go home and fetch the old ones," he said.

When Jussi jogged home, a few days later, in a shiny cart drawn by a grey mare, his parents ran to greet him. And after he'd related his adventures with the Devil, and they'd admired the boots on his feet, his father said fondly, "We missed you, Son. We knew you'd not fail us, though your brothers did."

"They'll not be back," said Jussi gently, for he knew his brothers better than the old people did. "But now you're coming home with me, to a new and prosperous farm."

Those who tell this tale say that Jussi and his parents lived in contentment many a year. And fame of his remarkable boots spread far and wide. "How did you get them?" people asked in wonder, once they'd stared and touched and sniffed at the sturdy black leather.

"By keeping my temper!" Jussi chortled.

To this day, men of Suomi talk of the boots made from the Devil's hide. "They never wore out," they say. "They're somewhere, tramping the countryside. No one knows who the wearer is, now. But he's lucky. For, like Jussi, with each step he scrunches the Evil One down, down, deeper into Hell."

# yann the fearless

## As retold by
### GENEVIEVE MASSIGNAN

*In which Yann comes into possession of a priest's stole, which makes him completely fearless. Protected by the stole, Yann frees several households of their ghosts. Then he sets off to Paris to free a King's daughter from her bond with the Devil!*

HE WAS a little boy who had lost his mother and father and was being brought up by his uncle, the priest. The little boy had no evil in him, but he was a little tricky to manage, if you like, and his uncle was not succeeding in teaching him any discipline.

Once when the priest had put Yann in the church as a punishment, he forgot that he was there, and the child had to stay there all night long. When he saw dusk approaching, he went into a confessional to get out of the cold.

At about midnight he heard a noise in the church. "Get that out of here!" said a voice.

"What is the matter with you?" replied Yann, who was not afraid.

Said the voice, "When I was a priest, I decided to steal something. I pinched the priest's stole, and I also took a golden goblet, and in order to hide them I put them in the priest's garden."

This was the previous priest of the parish. He was dead, and they had buried him under the flagstones of the church, as they still do sometimes.

The voice went on, "I had sworn on my life that I had not stolen them. I even said I would be happy to be damned forever if I was not telling the truth. Now I am in hell and know no rest. Do tell the present priest not to pray for me every Sunday, as is the custom, for I suffer more when prayers are said for me."

The next morning the sacristan went into the church to ring the Angelus and found Yann shut in there. Astounded, he went to tell the priest. "There is a robber in the church."

The priest came along, remembering then where he had left his nephew. "It is my fault," he said. "I shut the boy up in the church yesterday."

Yann told his uncle what the previous parish priest had said, remembering to mention that the things stolen from the church were buried in the priest's garden.

"Let us go and see at once!" said his uncle. They dug and searched in the garden and under the arbour, and they found what they were looking for. The priest kept the golden goblet and gave the stole to the boy. Yann had asked to have it, for the dead man had also said to him, "Keep the stole and you will never be afraid."

One day, when Yann was fifteen or sixteen, he said to himself, "With this stole I am sure of never being afraid. I am going around the world."

On his way he came upon an old house, an ancient castle which was crumbling into ruins and he asked if he could take shelter there for the night. "Yes," he was told, "if you will sleep in the room up there, but no one dares to go in because no one who does ever comes back."

"I will willingly sleep in that room." So he went in and lay down to rest, but all night long there was noise. It was as if a man were there wailing in great pain. "Why do you wail like that?" said Yann out loud.

"I hid stolen money in this castle. I wanted to give it back, but I died before I could." The dead man also told Yann where the stolen money was. It was in the cellar.

The next morning the landlord went to the room and opened the door. (He had locked Yann in the night before.)

The youth explained what had happened that night and where the dead man had hidden the stolen money. The landlord started searching the cellar with Yann. They dug under the castle and brought up a great deal of money. "As you found this money," the landlord said to the youth, "it will be yours. You have freed me at last from this dead man's cries of woe."

"I do not need it," said Yann. He took a little and went off saying, "The rest will be for the poor." So he went on his way.

He reached another house and asked to spend the

night there. He was told the same story.

"I have no room to give you except one where noises are heard all night. If you are not afraid, take it!" said the landlord.

"Ah," said Yann, "well, I'll keep an eye open and we'll see."

They gave him something to eat—bread and cider—so that he would stay awake. At midnight as he was warming himself by the fire he heard a noise in the chimney. "Make as much noise as you like! I am not afraid," said Yann. Shortly after he saw a leg fall down the chimney. "Well," said he, "here is a skittle. I will set it up." A moment later he again heard a noise, and there was another leg falling. "Well, well, well, now I have two skittles." Yann placed the two legs upright, one next to the other, and resumed his vigil by the fireplace. As the noise began again, he cried, "Go ahead, make as much noise as you like!" One after the other there fell an arm and a few minutes later another arm, which he set up next to the legs like skittles. Then the body of a man came down the chimney. Yann grabbed the body round the middle and put the legs and arms around the trunk. "Now for the head!" And sure enough a head fell in the fireplace. "Well, well, well! Here is a ball to play skittles with."

Yann sat down again by the fire, eating a piece of bread. Suddenly he turned round and saw to his surprise that the body stood up and was saying as it came back to life, "You are pretty fearless, Yann."

"You are the one who is fearless, as you have stolen my skittles!"

This corpse was a devil who had assumed this form in order to frighten everyone. But Yann calmly went to the table to eat, and said, "Come on and eat with me."

Then another devil arrived, then two, then three. They all went to the side of the table opposite Yann, and pushed the table over on him in order to crush him.

"Cut it out!" Yann said. "I have my grandfather's scarf right here. So you'd better watch out!"

The devils kept on surrounding and threatening him. There was one, a cripple, who was nastier than the others. Yann put the stole around his neck, the devil began to yell, and the others all left.

"Now, before I let you go," Yann said, "you'll have to sign this saying that you won't have any power over anyone in this house for the nine *lignées* (generations)."

But the devil didn't want to sign it at any price. So Yann tightened the stole around his neck, and forced him to sign what he wanted him to.

As he left, the devil shouted at him, "You've gone too far!" and he took a rock from the window-sill and threw it in Yann's face, which turned as black as the chimney—it was so bruised.

"If I ever meet you again, I'll sure make you watch your step!" Yann said in turn.

Once again he had rescued the household with whom

he had spent only one night. In acknowledgment, the owner offered him his daughter in marriage.

"No," Yann said, "I don't want to; I'm not going to get married." And once again he left and wandered around aimlessly. One day he heard that large numbers of people were gathering in Paris. In fact, long ago the Devil was promised that he would receive a king's daughter every fifty years; and now it was the turn of the King of France's own daughter to be surrendered to him.

Yann said to himself, "I have to go see the King first." Since travelling wasn't any problem for him, he went to Paris and said to the King, "Everyone is saying that the Devil is demanding your daughter."

"Alas, yes!" the King said.

"Let me stay close by her the night you have to hand her over, and I promise you I'll take care of the Devil. Believe me—if you do as I say, your daughter won't be taken away from you. Have a small vat placed in the middle of the large hall, and have it filled with holy water. You'll send for all the bishops, the archbishops, and even the Pope, and when everyone is gathered around the small vat, you'll have a *balai de cour* (farmyard broom) distributed to each one. When the last one of these important dignitaries enters the large hall, you'll see that he doesn't dare take a broom and go near the vat of holy water."

Yann's suggestions were carried out. Everything was in place on the appointed evening. The Devil appeared at the door of the hall; he immediately saw Yann and recognized him.

"Give me the King's daughter!" he said to him.

"Go and get her, if you want her!" Yann answered.

"Throw her over here to me!"

"Come and get her over here! If you want her, you'll come in this room to get her."

The Devil finally agreed to cross the threshold. Yann immediately threw the stole around his neck, and shouted to the bishops, the archbishops, and the Pope gathered around the vat: "Quick! Take your brooms and splash holy water on the Devil. Really give it to him! Don't be afraid."

And they all did as he said. The Devil was caught. Then Yann had him sign an agreement that from then on, for a hundred generations, he wouldn't have any right to any daughter of the King of France, and he added, "Before I release you, and as you blackened my face the last time we met, you're going to make me the most handsome boy there is."

The Devil made him the best-looking boy ever seen in the world. However, as he left, he again grabbed a stone that had fallen out of the palace wall (he had to take something everywhere he went!), but this time he didn't throw it at anyone, and then he disappeared.

When the King's daughter met her rescuer, she fell in love with him, and the King proposed to Yann that he become his son-in-law.

"No," the young man answered, "I won't get married

until I've faced another danger; I'm trying to learn what fear is."

Since the Princess very much wanted to marry him, she went and found one of these women who study the stars, to ask her how to frighten Yann.

The fortune-teller told her, "You only have to cook a loaf of bread, and when it's done, you dig out the inside and put in a blackbird, leaving it a little air so it won't die. Then you tell this young man to cut into this loaf of bread before leaving the palace, and you'll see: when the blackbird flies out, it'll scare him."

Yann was getting ready to leave the King's palace; the Princess came and said to him, "At least do me the favour of eating some of this bread that I've made for you before you leave."

"That, I won't refuse," he said. And as he cut into the crust, the blackbird suddenly flew out! Yann was so frightened that he fell over backwards.

The King's daughter went over to him and said, "You were scared!"

"Yes," he said.

"Well then, since you now know what fear is, there's nothing to keep us from getting married."

"You're right," said Yann. "I can't ever again take chances, since I've been afraid once in my life."

Remember that he was still wearing his stole in order not to be afraid, but this time he was taken by surprise.

Then Yann consented to marry the King's daughter, and later on he in turn became King.

# The Devil in the Churchyard

## A. E. COPPARD

*In which Shadrach, an old miser, having refused his
brother, Mark, fifty pounds, dies and is buried with his
fortune. One dark night the sexton and his friend go to
dig up the money. An old man, passing by, sees the
sexton's white smock and believes it to be a ghost . . . but
the tables are turned on the two thieves when they think
they see the Devil!*

"HENRY TURLEY was one of those awkward old chaps
as had more money than he knowed what to do wi'.
Shadrach we called him, the silly man. He had worked
for it, worked hard for it, but when he was old he stuck
to his fortune and wouldn't spend a sixpence of it on
his comforts. What a silly man!"

The thatcher, who was thus talking of Henry Turley
(long since dead and gone) in the "Black Cat" of Starn-
combe, was himself perhaps fifty years old. Already
there was a crank of age or of dampness or of mere
custom in most of his limbs, but he was bluff and gruff
and hale enough, with a bluffness of manner that could
only offend a fool—and fools never listened to him.

"Shadrach—that's what we called him—was a good
man wi' cattle, a masterpiece; he would strip a cow as

clean as a tooth and you never knowed a cow have a bad quarter as Henry Turley ever milked. And when he was buried he was buried with all that money in his coffin, holding it in his hands, I reckon.

"He had plenty of relations—you wouldn't know 'em, it is thirty years ago I be speaking of—but it was all down in black and white so's no one could touch it. A lot of people in these parts had a right to some of it, Jim Scarrott for one, and Issy Hawker a bit, Mrs. Keelson, poor woman, ought to have had a bit, and his own brother, Mark Turley; but he left it in the will as all his fortune was to be buried in the coffin along of him. 'Twas cruel, but so it is and so it will be, for whenever such people has a shilling to give away they goes and claps it on some fat pig's haunches. The foolishness! Sixty pounds it was, in a canister, and he held it in his hand."

"I don't believe a word of it," said a mild-faced man sitting in the corner. "Henry Turley never did a deed like that."

"What?" growled the thatcher with unusual ferocity.

"Coorse I'm not disputing what you're saying, but he never did such a thing in his life."

"Then you calls me a liar?"

"Certainly not. O no, don't misunderstand me, but Henry Turley never did any such thing, I can't believe it of him."

"Huh! I be telling you facts, and facts be true one

way or another. Now you waunts to call over me, you waunts to know the rights of everything and the wrongs of nothing."

"Well," said the mild-faced man, pushing his pot toward the teller of tales, "I might believe it to-morrow, but it's a bit of a twister now, this minute!"

"Ah, that's all right then"—the thatcher was completely mollified. "Well the worst part of the case was his brother Mark. Shadrach served him shameful, treated him like a dog. (Good health!) Ah, like a dog. Mark was older nor him, about seventy, and he lived by himself in a little house out by the hanging pust, not much of a cottage, it warn't—just wattle and daub wi' a thetch o' straa'—but the lease was running out ('twas a lifehold affair) and unless he bought this little house for fifty pound he'd got to go out of it. Well, old Mark hadn't got no fifty pounds, he was ate up wi' rheumatics and only did just a little light labour in the woods, they might as well a' asked him for the King's crown, so he said to his master: Would he lend him the fifty pounds?

" 'No, I can't do that,' his master says.

" 'You can deduct it from my wages,' Mark says.

" 'Nor I can't do that neither,' says his master, 'but there's your brother Henry, he's worth a power o' money, ask him.' So Mark asks Shadrach to lend him the fifty pounds, so's he could buy this little house. 'No,' says Henry, 'I can't.' Nor he wouldn't. Well—old Mark says to him: 'I doan wish you no harm, Henry,' he says, 'but I hope as how you'll die in a ditch.' (Good health!) And sure enough he did. That was his own brother, he were strooken wi' the sun and died in a ditch, Henry did, and when he was buried his fortune was buried with him, in a little canister, holding it in his hand, I reckons. And a lot of good that was to him! He hadn't been buried a month when two bad parties putt their heads together. Levi Carter, one was, he was the sexton, a man that was half a loony as I always thought. O yes, he had got all his wits about him, somewheres, only they didn't often get much of a quorum, still he got them—somewheres.

"T'other was a chap by the name of Impey, lived in Slack the shoemaker's house down by the old traveller's garden. He wasn't much of a mucher, helped in the fieldwork and did shepherding at odd times. And these two chaps made up their minds to goo and collar Henry Turley's fortune out of his coffin one night and share it between theirselves. 'Twas crime, ye know, might a been prison for life, but this Impey was a bad lot—he'd the manners of a pig, pooh! filthy!—and I expects he persuaded old Levi on to do it. Bad as body-snatchen, coorse 'twas!

"So they goos together one dark night, 'long in November it was, and well you knows, all of you, as well as I, that nobody can't ever see over our church-yard wall by day let alone on a dark night. You all knows that, don't you?" asserted the thatcher, who appeared to lay some stress upon this point in his narrative. There were murmurs of acquiescence by all except the mild-faced man, and the thatcher continued: " 'Twere about nine o'clock when they dug out the earth. 'Twarn't a very hard job, for Henry was only just a little way down. He was buried on top of his old woman, and she was on top of her two daughters. But when they got down to the coffin Impey didn't much care for that part of the job, he felt a little bit sick, so he gives the hammer and the screwdriver to Levi and he says; 'Levi,' he says, 'are you game to make a good job o' this?'

" 'Yes, I be,' says old Levi.

" 'Well, then,' Impey says, 'yous'll have my smock on now while I just creeps off to old Wannaker's sheep and collars one of they fat lambs over by the 'lotments.'

" 'You're not going to leave me here,' says Carter, 'what be I going to do?'

" 'You go on and finish this 'ere job, Levi,' he says, 'you get the money and put back all the earth and don't stir out of the yard afore I comes or I'll have yer blood.'

" 'No,' says Carter, 'you maun do that.'

" 'I 'ull do that,' Impey says, 'he've got some smartish lambs I can tell 'ee, fat as snails.'

" 'No,' says Carter, 'I waun't have no truck wi' that, tain't right.'

" 'You will,' says Impey, 'and I 'ull get the sheep. Here's my smock. I'll meet 'ee here again in ten minutes. I'll have that lamb if I 'as to cut his blasted head off.' And he rooshed away before Levi could stop him. So Carter putts on the smock and finishes the job. He got the money and putt the earth back on poor Henry and tidied it up, and then he went and sat in the church poorch waiting for this Impey to come back.

"Just as he did that an oldish man passed by the gate. He was coming to this very place for a drop o' drink and he sees old Levi's white figure sitting in the church poorch and it frittened him so that he took to his heels and tore along to this very room we be sittin' in now— only 'twas thirty years ago.

" 'What in the name of God's the matter wi' you?' they says to him, for he'd a face like chalk and his lips was blue as a whetstone. 'Have you seen a goost?'

" 'Yes,' he says, 'I have seen a goost, just now then.'

" 'A goost?' they says, 'a goost? You an't seen no goost.'

" 'I seen a goost.'

" 'Where a' you seen a goost?'

"So he told 'em he seen a goost sitting up in the church poorch.

" 'I shan't have that,' says old Mark Turley, for he was a-setting here.

" 'I tell you 'twas then,' says the man.

" 'Can't be nothing worse'n I be myself,' Mark says.

" 'I say as 'tis,' the man said, and he was vexed too. 'Goo and see for yourself.'

" 'I would goo too and all,' said old Mark, 'if only I could walk it, but my rheumatucks be that scrematious I can't walk it. Goosts! There's ne'er a mortal man as

ever see'd a goost. I'd go, my lad, if my legs 'ud stand it.'
And there was a lot of talk like that until a young
sailor spoke up—Irish he was, his name was Pat
Crowe, he was on furlough. I dunno what he was a-
doing in this part of the world, but there he was and he
says to Mark: 'If you be game enough, I be, and I'll
carry you up to the churchyard on my back.' A great
stropping feller he was. 'You will?' says Mark. 'That I
will,' he says. 'Well I be game for 'ee,' says Mark, and
so they ups him on to the sailor's shoulders like a sack
o' corn and away they goos, but not another one there
was man enough to goo with them.

"They went slogging up to the churchyard gate all
right, but when they got to staggering along 'tween the
gravestones Mark thought he could see a something
white sitting in the poorch, but the sailor couldn't see
anything at all with that lump on his shoulders.

" 'What's that there?' Mark whispered in Pat's ear.
And Pat Crowe whispers back, just for joking; 'Old
Nick in his nightshirt.'

" 'Steady now,' Mark whispers, 'go steady Pat, it's
getting up and coming.' Pat only gives a bit of a chuckle
and says; 'Ah, that's him, that's just like him.'

"Then Levi calls out from the poorch soft like: 'You
got him then! Is he a fat 'un?'

" 'Holy God,' cried the sailor, 'it *is* the devil!' and he
chucks poor Mark over his back at Levi's feet and runs
for his mortal life. He was the most frittened of the lot
'cos he hadn't believed in anything at all—but there

In Loving
Memory of
HENRY TURLEY
Bachelor of this
Parish Died 1890

In
Loving
Memory
of Mary
Burnam
Died in
1862 AD

it was. And just as he gets to the gate he sees someone else coming along in the dark carrying a something on its shoulder—it was Impey wi' the sheep. 'Powers above,' cried Pat Crowe, 'it's the Day of Judgment come for sartin!' And he went roaring the news up street like a madman, and Impey went off somewheres too—but I dunno where Impey went.

"Well, poor old Mark laid on the ground, he were a game old cock, but he could hardly speak, he was strook dazzled. And Levi was frittened out of his life in the darkness and couldn't make anythink out of nothink. He just creeps along to Mark and whispers: 'Who be that? Who be that?' And old Mark looks up very timid, for he thought his last hour was on him, and he says: 'Be that you, Satan?' Drackly Levi heard that—all in a onexpected voice he jumped quicker en my neighbour's flea. He gave a yell bigger nor Pat Crowe and he bolted too. But as he went he dropped the little tin canister and old Mark picked it up. And he shook the canister, and he heerd money in it, and then something began to dawn on him, for he knowed how his brother's fortune had been buried.

" 'I rede it, I rede it,' he says, 'that was Levi Carter, the dirty thief! I rede it, I rede it,' he says. And he putt the tin can in his pocket and hopped off home as if he never knowed what rheumatucks was at all. And when he opened that canister there was the sixty golden sovereigns in that canister. Sixty golden sovereigns! 'Bad things 'ull be worse afore they're better,' says

Mark, 'but they never won't be any better than this.'
And so he stuck to the money in the canister, and
that's how he bought his cottage arter all. 'Twarn't
much of a house, just wattle and daub, wi' a thetch o'
straa', but 'twas what he fancied, and there he ended
his days like an old Christian man. (Good health!)"

# THE DEVIL AND THE GUACHINANGO

JOSÉ LAKI

*In which a devil, disguised as a handsome young man, asks for the hand of the beautiful Piriang. But the devil gives himself away when he asks her to remove her cross. Piriang and her mother capture the devil in a large jar and pay a guachinango to bury the jar deep in the ground. The devil bargains with the guachinango to set him free . . .*

THERE ONCE lived in a suburb of a town a very religious old widow who had a beautiful daughter, Piriang by name. Young men from different parts of the town came to court Piriang, and the mother always preferred the rich to the poor. Whenever Piriang's friends told her that the man whom she rejected would have been a good match for her, she always answered that she would rather have a devil for a husband than such a man.

One day a devil heard Piriang giving this answer to one of her friends. Thus encouraged, he disguised himself as a young man of noble blood, and went to Piriang's house to offer her his love. The mother and daughter received this stranger with great civility, for

96

he appeared to them to be the son of a nobleman. In the richness of his dress he was unexcelled by his rivals. After he had been going to Piriang's house for a few weeks, the old widow told him one day to come prepared to be married on the following Tuesday. On the Sunday before the wedding-day he had a long conversation with Piriang. He calmly asked her to take off the cross that she had about her neck, for it made her look ugly, he said. She refused to do so, however, because she had worn this cross ever since she was a child. After he had departed, Piriang told her mother what he had asked her to do.

The next day the mother went to the church. She told the priest that Piriang's bridegroom had ordered her to take off her cross from her neck. The priest said that that man was a devil; for no man, as a son of God, would say that a cross made the one who wore it look ugly. The priest gave the mother a small image of the Virgin Mary. He instructed her to show the image to the bridegroom. If when he beheld it he turned his back on her as she was holding it, she was to tie him around the neck with her *cintas* — a holy belt worn by women. Then she was to put him in a large jar, and bury him at least twenty-one feet under the ground.

The mother went home very much distressed because she had allowed her daughter to become engaged to a devil. She told Piriang not to talk with her bridegroom, because she feared that he was a devil. That night he came with his friend dressed like him. The mother was very gracious to them. They talked about the wedding. When the old woman held up the image of the Virgin Mary the two men turned their backs on her. She immediately wound her *cintas* around the neck of her daughter's bridegroom, and Piriang came in with the dried tail of a sting-ray in her right hand. She whipped him with this as hard as she could. Then the two together forced him to get into a large jar. After warning him not to come back to earth again, the old woman covered the jar with a piece of cloth wet with holy water. The other devil suddenly disappeared.

The next morning a guachinango—a vagabond— happened to pass by the house of the old woman. She called him in, showed him the jar, and told him to bury it at least twenty-one feet deep. When he asked how much she would pay him, she promised to give him ten pesos. He agreed: so, putting the jar on his right shoulder, he set out. When he reached a quiet place, he heard whispers behind him. He stopped and looked around, but could see nothing. Then he put the jar on the ground to rest a few minutes. Now he discovered that the whispers were coming from inside the jar. He was very much surprised.

"What are you?" asked the guachinango. "Are you a man, or a devil?"

"I am a devil, my friend," answered the voice. "The old woman forced me to go into this jar. Be kind to me, my friend, and liberate me!"

"I shall obey the old woman in order to get my pay,"

said the guachinango. "I will bury you even deeper than twenty-one feet."

"If you will bury me just three feet deep," said the devil, "I will give you a large sum of money."

"I will bury you just one-and-a-half feet deep, if you can give me much money," said the guachinango.

"I will give you five hundred pesos," said the devil. "Dig the ground near the stump of that mabolo-tree. There you will find the money in a dirty black purse."

After the guachinango had buried the devil, he went to the mabolo-tree and took the money. Then he went to the nearest village and played casino. As soon as he lost all his money, he returned to the devil. "I have lost all the money you gave me," he said. "I will now bury you twenty-one feet deep."

"No, do not bury me so deep as that, my friend!" said the devil calmly. "I can give you twice as much money as I gave you before. You will find it in the same place that you found the other."

The guachinango took the money and went to the village again to gamble. Again he lost. He returned to the devil, and asked him angrily why he always lost the money he gave him. "I don't know," answered the devil. "I have given you fifteen hundred pesos, but you haven't even a cent now. You ought to set me free at once."

"Aha! I won't let you go," said the guachinango. "I will bury you thirty-nine feet now."

"I have a plan in mind," said the devil, "which will

benefit you extremely; but before I explain my plan,
let me ask you if you would like to marry the daughter
of the king."

"I have a great desire to be king some day," said the
guachinango; "but how can you make me the husband
of a princess, when you are only a devil, and I am
nothing but a poor guachinango?"

"As soon as you set me free," said the devil, "I will
enter the mouth of the princess and go into her brains.
Then I will give her a very painful headache which no
physician can cure. The king will make an announce-
ment saying that he who can cure his daughter of her
disease shall marry her. When you hear this announce-
ment, go to the palace at once, and offer your services
to the king. As soon as you reach the princess, tell me
that you have come, and I will leave her immediately.
The princess will then recover her former health, and
you will be married to her. Do not fail to go to the
palace, for I am determined to reward you for your
kindness to me."

After the guachinango had liberated the devil, he
immediately set out for the city. He had not been there
three days when he met a group of soldiers crying that
"he who could cure the princess should have her to
wife." The guachinango stopped the soldiers, and said
that he could cure the princess. They took him before
the king, where a written agreement was made. If he
could not cure the princess in three days, he should
lose his life; but if he cured her by the end of the third

day, he should marry her. The guachinango was then conducted to the room of the princess. When he approached her, he said to the devil that he had come. "You must leave the princess now; for, if you don't, I shall be executed." But the devil refused to leave, because he wanted to get revenge. He further told the guachinango that he wanted him to die, for then his soul would go to hell.

The guachinango became more and more hopeless. On the morning of the third day he thought of a good plan to get rid of his enemy. He asked the king to order all the bells of the neighbouring churches to be tolled, while every one in the palace was to cry out loud, "Here she comes!" While all this noise was going on, the guachinango approached the princess, and told the devil that the old woman was coming with her *cintas*. When the devil heard this, he was terribly frightened, and left the princess and disappeared. The next day the guachinango was married to the princess.

# TNE GREEN ROBE

*Re-told from a story by*
WILLIAM J. THOMS

*In which a poor young man makes a pact with the devil for riches. In return for not washing or combing his hair for seven years, and promising his soul to the devil if he dies within that time, the devil presents him with a green robe whose magic pockets are always full of gold.*

ONCE UPON a time there were three brothers. The two elder ones hated their younger brother, so when they all went out into the world to seek their fortunes they told him to go his own way. "We don't want you with us; you will have to travel by yourself." So they left him to his own devices.

The young brother walked for miles and miles, and eventually reached a very high mountain with a circle of trees at the top. He was starving with hunger, and he sat down under the trees and wept with despair. Suddenly he heard a loud noise: the Devil with his cloven hoof appeared before him, wearing a green robe. The Devil asked why he was crying and the young man told him all his troubles and how his brothers had abandoned him.

When the Devil heard this he said: "Well, I can help you. Put on this green robe. Its pockets are always full of gold, no matter how much you spend. But there is one condition: for seven years you must not wash yourself or comb your hair or say your prayers. And if you die during the seven years your soul will be mine. If you live, you will be free and a rich man for the rest of your life."

The young man had to agree to the Devil's terms or he would have starved to death. So he put on the green robe, and when he put his hands in the pockets he found them full of gold.

And so he went out into the world with his wonderful robe. For the first year things went well: he bought whatever he wanted and his appearance was reasonably tolerable to his friends. But by the second year his hair had grown so long that nobody recognised him, and he looked so dirty and unkempt that no one would invite him to their home. Each year things got worse, but he still gave alms to the poor and asked them to pray for him, that he would not die within the seven years and have to give his soul to the devil.

During the fourth year he came to an inn: at first the landlord would not give him lodgings, but then he saw the pockets full of gold and changed his mind. In the middle of the night Green Robe heard someone moaning bitterly in the next room. He went to see what was wrong, and found a miserable old man, who told him to go away as no one could help him. Green

Robe asked what was wrong. The old man told him he was in the landlord's debt, as he had no money, and the landlord wouldn't let him leave until he had paid.

"I have plenty of money," said Green Robe. "Let me pay for you." So he did, and saved the old man from his debt.

This old man had three beautiful daughters, and he told Green Robe he could marry one of them in return for his kindness. When they arrived at the old man's home, the two eldest daughters would have nothing to do with him as he looked so frightful. But the youngest said: "Dear Father, as this man helped you when you needed it, and you made him a promise, I will do whatever you ask." Green Robe took a ring from his finger, broke it in half, gave her one half and kept the other for himself. In her half of the ring he wrote his name, and in his half hers. And he said to her: "Take care of my ring. I must leave you now for three years. Be faithful to me, and I will return and marry you. But if at the end of three years I don't come back, you are free to marry someone else, for you will know that I am dead. While I am gone pray for me, that I shall return to you."

During the three years the two elder sisters mocked and laughed at the youngest, saying that she was going to have a bear for a husband instead of a man. But she ignored them, and told herself: "We should obey our father, whatever he asks of us."

Meanwhile Green Robe journeyed all over the world, buying beautiful presents for his betrothed. He did all kinds of good deeds and gave money to the poor. And he was rewarded, for at the end of the three years he was still alive and healthy. He went back to the circle of trees on the high mountain. The loud noise came again and the Devil appeared, angry to see him still alive. He threw back the young man's own robe, and demanded the Green Robe back. The young man was quite happy to give it back: he was free again and a rich man forever. He went home, washed and cut his hair, and set off to see his betrothed.

Her father met him at the door. He announced himself as the bridegroom, but the old man did not recognise him now that he was clean and his hair was cut, and he would not believe him. So he went to his future bride, but she would not believe him either. Then he asked her if she still had half of his ring. She fetched it, and when he produced the other half she saw how they matched, and realised that he was indeed her bridegroom.

Seeing what a good and handsome young man he was, the girl fell deeply in love with him. They were married at once. The two elder sisters were so angry that they had turned down such good fortune that on the day of the wedding one hanged herself and the other drowned.

That night a loud knocking was heard. The bridegroom went to open the door and found the Devil in

his Green Robe. The Devil seemed rather pleased with himself and said: "It's all worked out for the best after all: I now have two souls instead of just your own!"

# THE DEVIL

## GUY DE MAUPASSANT

*In which a peasant is forced to hire a washerwoman to sit with his dying mother while he tends to the harvest. Miser that he is, he begrudges the money that he must pay the woman and, fearing that his mother will linger on for weeks, bargains for a fixed price, however long it takes. But the old washerwoman has her own method of ensuring that she gets the better bargain!*

THE PEASANT was standing opposite the doctor, by the bedside of the dying old woman, and she, calmly resigned and quite lucid, looked at them and listened to their talking. She was going to die and she did not rebel at it, for her life was over—she was ninety-two.

The July sun streamed in at the window and through the open door and cast its hot flames onto the uneven brown clay floor which had been stamped down by four generations of clodhoppers. The smell of the fields came in also, driven by the brisk wind and parched by the noontide heat. The grasshoppers chirped themselves hoarse, filling the air with their shrill noise, like that of the wooden crickets which are sold to children at fair time.

111

The doctor raised his voice and said: "Honoré, you cannot leave your mother in this state; she may die at any moment." And the peasant, in great distress, replied: "But I must get in my wheat, for it has been lying on the ground a long time, and the weather is just right for it; what do you say about it, Mother?" And the dying woman, still possessed by her Norman avariciousness, replied yes with her eyes and her forehead and so urged her son to get in his wheat and to leave her to die alone. But the doctor got angry and, stamping his foot, he said: "You are no better than a brute; do you hear? And I will not allow you to do it. Do you understand? And if you must get in your wheat today, go and fetch Rapet's wife and make her look after your mother. I *will* have it. And if you do not obey me I will let you die like a dog when you are ill in your turn; do you hear me?"

The peasant, a tall thin fellow with slow movements who was tormented by indecision, by his fear of the doctor and his keen love for saving, hesitated, calculated and stammered out: "How much does La Rapet charge for attending sick people?"

"How should I know?" the doctor cried. "That depends upon how long she is wanted for. Settle it with her, by Jove! But I want her to be here within an hour; do you hear?"

So the man made up his mind. "I will go for her," he replied; "don't get angry, Doctor." And the latter left, calling out as he went: "Take care, you know, for I do not joke when I am angry!" And as soon as they were alone the peasant turned to his mother and said in a resigned voice: "I will go and fetch La Rapet, as the man *will* have it. Don't go off while I am away."

And he went out in his turn.

La Rapet, who was an old washerwoman, watched the dead and the dying of the neighbourhood, and then as soon as she had sewn her customers into that linen cloth from which they would emerge no more, she went and took up her irons to smooth the linen of the living. Wrinkled like a last year's apple, spiteful, envious, avaricious with a phenomenal avarice, bent double, as if she had been broken in half across the loins by the constant movement of the iron over the linen, one might have said that she had a kind of monstrous and cynical affection for a death struggle. She never spoke of anything but of the people she had seen die, of the various kinds of deaths at which she had been present, and she related, with the greatest minuteness, details which were always the same, just like a sportsman talks of his shots.

When Honoré Bontemps entered her cottage he found her preparing the starch for the collars of the village women, and he said: "Good evening; I hope you are pretty well, Mother Rapet."

She turned her head round to look at him and said: "Fairly well, fairly well, and you?"

"Oh, as for me, I am as well as I could wish, but my

mother is very sick."

"Your mother?"

"Yes, my mother!"

"What's the matter with her?"

"She is going to turn up her toes; that's what's the matter with her!"

The old woman took her hands out of the water and asked with sudden sympathy: "Is she as bad as all that?"

"The doctor says she will not last till morning."

"Then she certainly is very bad!" Honoré hesitated, for he wanted to make a few preliminary remarks before coming to his proposal, but as he could hit upon nothing, he made up his mind suddenly.

"How much are you going to ask to stop with her till the end? You know that I am not rich, and I cannot even afford to keep a servant girl. It is just that which has brought my poor mother to this state, too much work and fatigue! She used to work for ten, in spite of her ninety-two years. You don't find any made of that stuff nowadays!"

La Rapet answered gravely: "There are two prices: forty sous by day and three francs by night for the rich, and twenty sous by day and forty by night for the others. You shall pay me the twenty and forty." But the peasant reflected, for he knew his mother well. He knew how tenacious of life, how vigorous and unyielding she was. He knew, too, that she might last another week, in spite of the doctor's opinion, and so he said resolutely: "No, I would rather you would fix a price until the end. I will take my chance one way or the other. The doctor says she will die very soon. If that happens, so much the better for you and so much the worse for me, but if she holds out till tomorrow or longer, so much the better for me and so much the worse for you!"

The nurse looked at the man in astonishment, for she had never treated a death as a speculative job, and she hesitated, tempted by the idea of the possible gain. But almost immediately she suspected that he wanted to juggle her. "I can say nothing until I have seen your mother," she replied.

"Then come with me and see her."

She washed her hands and went with him immediately. They did not speak on the road; she walked with short, hasty steps, while he strode on with his long legs, as if he were crossing a brook at every step. The cows lying down in the fields, overcome by the heat, raised their heads heavily and lowed feebly at the two passers-by, as if to ask them for some green grass.

When they got near the house Honoré Bentemps murmured: "Suppose it is all over?" And the unconscious wish that it might be so showed itself in the sound of his voice.

But the old woman was not dead. She was lying on her back on her wretched bed, her hands covered with a pink cotton counterpane—horribly thin, knotty paws, like some strange animal's or like crabs' claws, hands closed by rheumatism, fatigue and the work of nearly a century which she had accomplished.

La Rapet went up to the bed and looked at the dying woman, felt her pulse, tapped her on the chest, listened to her breathing and asked her questions so as to hear her speak; then, having looked at her for some time longer, she went out of the room, followed by Honoré. His decided opinion was that the old woman would not last out the night, and he asked: "Well?" And the sick nurse replied: "Well, she may last two days, perhaps three. You will have to give me six francs, everything included."

"Six francs! Six francs!" he shouted. "Are you out of your mind? I tell you that she cannot last more than five or six hours!" And they disputed angrily for some time, but as the nurse said she would go home as the time was slipping away, and as his wheat would not come to the farmyard of its own accord, he agreed to her terms at last.

"Very well then, that is settled; six francs, including everything, until the corpse is taken out."

"That is settled, six francs."

And he went away with long strides to the wheat which was lying on the ground under the hot sun which ripens the grain, while the nurse returned to the house.

She had brought some work with her, for she worked without stopping by the side of the dead and dying, sometimes for herself, sometimes for the family who employed her as seamstress also, paying her rather more in that capacity. Suddenly she asked:

"Have you received the last sacrament, Mother Bontemps?"

The old peasant woman said no with her head, and La Rapet, who was very devout, got up quickly.

"Good heavens, is it possible? I will go and fetch the curé," and she rushed off to the parsonage so quickly that the urchins in the street thought some accident had happened when they saw her trotting off like that.

The priest came immediately in his surplice, preceded by a choirboy, who rang a bell to announce the passage of the Host through the parched and quiet country. Some men, working at a distance, took off their large hats and remained motionless until the white vestment had disappeared behind some farm buildings; the women who were making up the sheaves stood up to make the sign of the cross; the frightened black hens ran away along the ditch until they reached a well-known hole through which they suddenly disappeared, while a foal, which was tied up in a meadow, took fright at the sight of the surplice and began to gallop round at the length of its rope, kicking violently. The choirboy, in his red cassock, walked quickly, and the priest, the square biretta on his bowed head, followed him, muttering some prayers. Last of all came La Rapet, bent almost double, as if she wished to prostrate herself; she walked with folded hands, as if she were in church.

Honoré saw them pass in the distance, and he asked: "Where is our priest going to?" And his man, who was more acute, replied: "He is taking the sacrament to your mother, of course!"

The peasant was not surprised and said: "That is quite possible," and went on with his work.

Mother Bontemps confessed, received absolution and extreme unction, and the priest took his departure, leaving the two women alone in the suffocating cottage. La Rapet began to look at the dying woman and to ask herself whether it could last much longer.

The day was on the wane, and a cooler air came in stronger puffs, making a picture of Epinal, which was fastened to the wall by two pins, flap up and down. The scanty window curtains, which had formerly been white but were now yellow and covered with flyspecks, looked as if they were going to fly off and seemed to struggle to get away, like the old woman's soul.

Lying motionless, with her eyes open, the old mother seemed to await the death which was so near and which yet delayed its coming, with perfect indifference. Her short breath whistled in her throat. It would stop altogether soon, and there would be one woman less in the world—one whom nobody would regret.

At nightfall Honoré returned, and when he went up to the bed and saw that his mother was still alive he asked: "How is she?" just as he had done formerly when she had been sick. Then he sent La Rapet away, saying to her: "Tomorrow morning at five o'clock without fail." And she replied: "Tomorrow at five o'clock."

She came at daybreak and found Honoré eating his soup, which he had made himself, before going to work.

"Well, is your mother dead?" asked the nurse.

"She is rather better, on the contrary," he replied with a malignant look out of the corners of his eyes. Then he went out.

La Rapet was seized with anxiety and went up to the dying woman, who was in the same state, lethargic and impassive, her eyes open and her hands clutching the counterpane. The nurse perceived that this might go on thus for two days, four nights, eight days, even, and her avaricious mind was seized with fear. She was excited to fury against the cunning fellow who had tricked her and against the woman who would not die.

Nevertheless, she began to sew and waited with her eyes fixed on the wrinkled face of Mother Bontemps. When Honoré returned to breakfast he seemed quite satisfied and even in a bantering humour, for he was carrying in his wheat under very favourable circumstances.

La Rapet was getting exasperated; every passing minute now seemed to her so much time and money stolen from her. She felt a mad inclination to choke this old ass, this headstrong old fool, this obstinate old wretch—to stop that short, rapid breath, which was robbing her of her time and money—by squeezing

her throat a little. But then she reflected on the danger of doing so, and other thoughts came into her head, so she went up to the bed and said to her: "Have you ever seen the devil?"

Mother Bontemps whispered: "No."

Then the sick nurse began to talk and to tell her tales likely to terrify her weak and dying mind. "Some minutes before one dies the devil appears," she said, "to all. He has a broom in his hand, a saucepan on his head, and he utters loud cries. When anybody has seen him all is over, and that person has only a few moments longer to live"; and she enumerated all those to whom the devil had appeared that year: Josephine Loisel, Eulalie Ratier, Sophie Padagnau, Séraphine Grospied.

Mother Bontemps, who was at last most disturbed in mind, moved about, wrung her hands and tried to turn her head to look at the other end of the room. Suddenly La Rapet disappeared at the foot of the bed. She took a sheet out of the cupboard and wrapped herself up in it; then she put the iron pot onto her head so that its three short, bent feet rose up like horns, took a broom in her right hand and a tin pail in her left, which she threw up suddenly so that it might fall to the ground noisily.

Certainly when it came down it made a terrible noise. Then, climbing onto a chair, the nurse showed herself, gesticulating and uttering shrill cries into the pot which covered her face, while she menaced the old peasant woman, who was nearly dead, with her broom.

Terrified, with a mad look on her face, the dying woman made a superhuman effort to get up and escape; she even got her shoulders and chest out of bed; then she fell back with a deep sigh. All was over, and La Rapet calmly put everything back into its place; the broom into the corner by the cupboard, the sheet inside it, the pot onto the hearth, the pail onto the floor and the chair against the wall. Then with a professional air she closed the dead woman's enormous eyes, put a plate on the bed and poured some holy water into it, dipped the twigs of boxwood into it and, kneeling down, she fervently repeated the prayers for the dead, which she knew by heart, as a matter of business.

When Honoré returned in the evening, he found her praying. He calculated immediately that she had made twenty sous out of him, for she had only spent two days and one night there, which made five francs altogether, instead of the six which he owed her.

# ḣOW ṪΗE ΔEVIL
# MARRIEΔ ṪΗREE SISṪERS

*edited by*

STITH THOMPSON

*In which the Devil, in the guise of a handsome young man, marries in turn three sisters. The first two are imprisoned in Hell for their disobedience, but the third outwits her husband and saves them all—and thus the Devil loses his taste for marriage!*

ONCE UPON a time the Devil was seized with a desire to marry. He therefore left Hell, took the form of a handsome young man, and built a fine large house. When it was completed and furnished in the most fashionable style, he introduced himself to a family where there were three pretty daughters, and paid his addresses to the eldest of them. The handsome man pleased the maiden, her parents were glad to see a daughter so well provided for, and it was not long before the wedding was celebrated.

When he had taken his bride home he presented her with a tastefully arranged bouquet, led her through all the rooms of the house, and finally to a closed door. "The whole house is at your disposal," said he, "only I must request one thing of you; that is, that you do not on any account open this door."

Of course the young wife promised faithfully, but equally, of course, she could scarcely wait for the moment to come when she might break her promise. When the Devil had left the house the next morning, under pretence of going hunting, she ran hastily to the forbidden door, opened it and saw a terrible abyss full of fire that shot up towards her, and singed the flowers on her bosom. When her husband came home and asked her whether she had kept her promise, she unhesitatingly said "Yes"; but he saw by the flowers that she was telling a lie, and said: "Now I will not put your curiosity to the test any longer. Come with me, I will show you myself what is behind the door." Thereupon he led her to the door, opened it, gave her such a push that she fell down into Hell, and shut the door again.

A few months after, he wooed the next sister for his wife, and won her; but with her everything that had happened with the first wife was exactly repeated.

Finally he courted the third sister. She was a prudent maiden, and said to herself: "He has certainly murdered my two sisters; but then it is a splendid match for me, so I will try and see whether I cannot be more fortunate than they." And accordingly she consented. After the wedding the bridegroom gave her a beautiful bouquet, but forbade her, also, to open the door which he pointed out.

Not a whit less curious than her sisters, she too opened the forbidden door when the Devil had gone

hunting, but she had previously put her flowers in water. Then she saw behind the door the fatal abyss and her sisters therein. "Ah!" she exclaimed, "poor creature that I am; I thought I had married an ordinary man, and instead of that he is the Devil! How can I get away from him?" She carefully pulled her two sisters out of hell and hid them. When the Devil came home he immediately looked at the bouquet which she again wore on her bosom, and when he found the flowers so fresh he asked no questions; but reassured as to his secret, he now, for the first time, really loved her.

After a few days she asked him if he would carry three chests for her to her parents' house, without putting them down or resting on the way. "But," she added, "you must keep your word, for I shall be watching you." The Devil promised to do exactly as she wished. So the next morning she put one of her sisters in a chest, and laid it on her husband's shoulders. The Devil, who is very strong, but also very lazy and unaccustomed to work, soon got tired of carrying the heavy chest, and wanted to rest before he was out of the street on which he lived; but his wife called out to him: "Don't put it down; I see you!" The Devil went reluctantly on with the chest until he had turned the corner, and then said to himself: "She cannot see me here; I will rest a little." But scarcely had he begun to put the chest down when the sister inside cried out: "Don't put it down; I see you still!"

Cursing, he dragged the chest on into another street, and was going to lay it down on a doorstep, but he again heard the voice: "Don't lay it down, you rascal; I see you still!" "What kind of eyes must my wife have," he thought, "to see around corners as well as straight ahead, and through walls as if they were made of glass!" and thus thinking he arrived, all in a perspiration and quite tired out, at the house of his mother-in-law, to whom he hastily delivered the chest, and then hurried home to strengthen himself with a good breakfast.

The same thing was repeated the next day with the second chest. On the third day his wife herself was to be taken home in the chest. She therefore prepared a figure which she dressed in her own clothes, and placed on the balcony, under the pretext of being able to watch him better; slipped quickly into the chest, and had the maid put it on the Devil's back. "The deuce!" said he; "this chest is a great deal heavier than the others; and today, when she is watching from the balcony, I shall have so much the less chance to rest."

So by dint of the greatest exertions he carried it, without stopping, to his mother-in-law, and then hastened home to breakfast scolding, and with his back almost broken. But quite contrary to custom, his wife did not come out to meet him, and there was no breakfast ready. "Margerita, where are you?" he cried; but received no answer. As he was running through the corridors he at length looked out of a window, and saw the figure on the balcony. "Margerita, have you gone to sleep? Come down. I am as tired as a dog, and as hungry as a wolf." But there was no reply. "If you do not come down instantly I will go up and bring you down," he cried, angrily; but Margerita did not stir. Enraged, he hastened up to the balcony, and gave her such a box on the ear that her head flew off, and he saw that the head was nothing but a milliner's form, and the body a bundle of rags. Raging, he rushed down and rummaged through the whole house, but in vain; he found only his wife's empty jewel-box. "Ha!" he cried; "she has been stolen from me, and her jewels, too!" and he immediately ran to inform her parents of the misfortune. But when he came near the house, to his great surprise he saw on the balcony above the door all three sisters, his wives, who were looking down on him with scornful laughter.

Three wives at once terrified the Devil so much that he took his flight with all possible speed.

Since that time he has lost his taste for marrying.

# Ṫ∏Є ꙄṪȮꙆЄṆ ∏ЄꙂꙄ

## GODFRIED BOMANS

*In which a poor fisherman trades his heart and soul to the devil in return for riches. But the fisherman's family would rather have a father with feelings than all the wealth in the world, so the youngest son sets off to get back his father's heart.*

ONCE UPON a time there was a very poor fisherman. He had a wife and six children and a seventh was on the way. They lived together in a little house on the shore of a lake, and every morning the fisherman cast his nets, but since he caught little, his family was usually hungry. And because he loved his wife and children very much this made him sad.

One evening the fisherman hauled in his nets and looked gloomily at his catch.

"That is not good," he said. "If only I could catch more."

"You could," said a voice behind him.

The fisherman turned and saw a fine gentleman. He was sitting in a coach and blowing on his hands as if he felt cold. The fisherman shivered, for he too was suddenly very cold.

"Who are you?" he asked.

The gentleman smiled. But his eyes did not smile and he continued to look sharply at the fisherman.

"I will not tell you," he said. "Sell me your soul and you shall wallow in riches."

"How can I sell my soul?" asked the fisherman.

"You have only to breathe into my mouth. Then it will be done."

"And what shall I get for it?"

"Everything."

The fisherman thought. And as he thought, it was as if a cold wind blew about him.

"You are the Devil!" he exclaimed.

The man in the coach bit his lip. The smile died on his face and his eyes flashed.

"Sell me your soul," he said, "and you shall wallow in riches."

"All right," said the fisherman.

The gentleman stepped down from the coach and stood before the fisherman.

"Open your mouth," he said, "and blow your breath into mine."

The fisherman blew his breath into the stranger's mouth and at the same moment he felt a chill where his heart belonged.

"What have you done to my heart?" he asked fearfully.

The stranger smiled. His wan cheeks were suddenly tinged with pink and he looked at his frozen fingertips.

"They are tingling already," he said, "and I can feel life coming into my feet as well. In ten years you can recall me. If you want me, I will come, but you will not want me. You will have had your reward."

He jumped into the coach and whipped up the horses. The fisherman watched him until he was out of sight and then rolled up his net to go home. But in the meshes of the net he saw an oyster. He opened the shell and inside it he found a great, gleaming pearl. He put it in his trouser pocket and went home. The children were sitting at the table and his wife was leaning over the cradle, for the new baby had just been born. She threw her arms round his neck and kissed him. Then she stepped back.

"How cold you are!" she cried in amazement.

The fisherman unloosed her arms and pushed her away from him.

"Call the mayor," he said shortly. "I have found a pearl."

The mayor came. And when he saw the pearl lying on the table he had difficulty in hiding his excitement, for it was the largest pearl he had ever seen.

"Not bad," he said casually, "but still only middling. I will give you a piece of land for it."

The fisherman exchanged the pearl for a piece of land that was no larger than the garden behind his own little house. But next day, when he put his spade into the ground, he struck the lid of an iron chest. And once again he went to the mayor and said: "I have found treasure."

This time the mayor did not dare to say that it was not much, for the chest was full of diamonds and precious jewels and only the king was rich enough to buy the treasure. In return for the jewels, the king gave the fisherman three ships, each with a hundred sailors on board.

The ships sailed off with a great fleet of other merchant ships, but in the middle of the ocean a mighty storm blew up, so that half the fleet sank beneath the waves. But the three ships were among those spared. The remainder were taken by pirates. They plundered the holds, drove the sailors overboard and set fire to the rest. Only the three ships which belonged to the fisherman escaped and returned to land filled with grain.

There was famine in the land, because nearly the whole fleet had been lost. The fisherman sold his grain for ten times its price and now he really was wallowing in riches, but he did nothing for his family. He bought the king's palace, leaving the king a single room for himself. The fisherman sat on the balcony in a straw hat and smoked cigars in the sunshine, for he no longer had anything to do. In the street below the balcony people stood and begged for bread. But the fisherman laughed at them.

"If you can pay for it!" he shouted down to them. "Not otherwise!"

.This was too much for the king. After all, he was

still king. He came to the fisherman in his dressing-gown and said:

"Listen, this cannot go on. All the people are dying, and soon I shall have no more subjects."

The men down in the street held their breath. What the king had said was true and they had never thought of it before.

"What is that to me?" answered the fisherman. "I am comfortable here and I want for nothing."

Then the king grew angry. He had never been angry in his life before, but now he was.

"Do you know what is wrong with you?" he cried. "You have no heart!"

The fisherman turned pale. "How did you know that?" he whispered.

"A child could see it," said the king. "The people are falling down dead in the street and here you sit on your balcony, smoking cigars. I call that heartless. For what am I to live on if no-one pays taxes? It looks to me as if you have sold your soul to the Devil."

The fisherman turned as white as a sheet. "How did you know that?" he asked again.

Now the king was frightened. "What!" he cried. "You didn't *really* do that, did you?"

The fisherman stared silently at the marble floor. "Yes," he said at last. "And that is why I sit in the sun all day. I am cold. Feel."

He took the king's hand and laid it on his chest. The king snatched his hand away quickly, as if he had touched a piece of ice.

"Go away," he said. "I do not want to see you here any more."

And he went to the edge of the balcony and leaned over the railing.

"My people," he said, "this man has sold his soul to the Devil. He is leaving my palace now and coming down. Let him go unhindered. No-one is to touch him. And the grain will be distributed among you."

The fisherman came out through the door into the street and the people gave way before him. Not a word was spoken, not a hand lifted against him. As he walked through the town, everywhere the shutters were pulled tight and the doors locked. When he tried to greet someone, the other would drop his eyes and pass quickly by. The news that he had sold his soul to the Devil flew from mouth to mouth as if on wings. The children stayed indoors wherever he appeared, and if he rang at a door to ask for bread the door remained shut. And although his pockets were full of gold, he had nothing to eat. Then he remembered his wife and children and went back to them—not because he loved them, but because he was hungry.

It was night by the time he reached his house. The children were sitting at the table and his wife was giving them their food. She ran to him and threw her arms round his neck. But he pushed her away.

"Don't you love me any more?" she asked softly.

"No," he said.

She came to him again and laid her head on his breast. Then she shrank back, for she felt the cold against her cheek.

"Then it is true," she whispered in horror. "I did not believe it."

"It is true," he said. "Send the children to bed, for I must eat."

The children went silently upstairs and the man without a heart sat down at the table and ate. When he had eaten he leaned forward in his chair and looked at her.

"Our troubles are over," he said. "We have money enough."

"Oh, yes," said his wife, "but you do not love me any more."

"That is true," said the man. "That was the price."

"What use is money," asked his wife, "if you can buy nothing for it?"

"The people will grow used to me," said the man, "and then their doors will be open again."

"Oh, yes. But what you get will bring you no happiness. Come, look at your fine new son. He will warm your heart for you. There is something wonderful about him too: he has a birthmark like a flame over his own heart."

She picked up the seventh child from the cradle and held it before his eyes. The man felt no desire to see his seventh child.

"I do not care," he said. "But that was the price."

The child grew quickly—a boy named John. When he was nearly ten years old he heard from his brothers what had happened and began to think about it. He understood why the house was so quiet and why their father never gave them a good-night kiss when they went to bed. And he understood why there was always plenty of food on the table, although his father never worked, but sat silently in his chair looking out of the window. He understood, too, why no visitors came and why everybody avoided the house. One day he even knew why there was a fiery red birthmark on his chest, for all that had happened just when he was born. And he took pity on his father and went to him.

"Father," he said, "is it true that you have no heart?"

"It is true," said his father. "But that was the price."

"Do you want to have it back again?" asked the boy.

His father looked at him in silence. "I want nothing," he said at last, "for I have no heart."

"Would you like me to bring it back?"

"I would like nothing," said his father. "How can I like anything?"

"The ten years are nearly over. You were promised that after ten years you could see the Devil again if you wished."

"How can I wish for anything?" said the father. "I sit here and wait for death. But do what your heart tells you. You still have one."

So, the boy prepared for a journey, for the day of his tenth birthday was approaching. He embraced his brothers and sisters and gave his mother a kiss. Then he went to his father and asked:

"Have you anything to tell me?"

"Nothing," said the man, "for I do not even remember your name."

"My name is John," said the boy. "Give me your hand, at least, for I have a difficult journey ahead of me."

"Why should I?" said his father. "Go along."

So John went out into the wide world in search of the Devil. He had only a little time left, for his birthday was the day after next, but many things can happen in two days.

On the evening of the first day he came to an inn. The people were very friendly and wondered that so young a boy should be abroad quite alone. While his bed was being prepared upstairs he stayed down in the taproom eating his supper. He listened to what the other guests were saying and after a while the talk came round to a man who had changed greatly in the last ten years. Before that he had never spoken a word to a soul, but suddenly he had changed. He had become lively and talkative and above all he loved children, although he had none himself. Yet people did not trust him, for he lived quite alone. But what surprised people most was that he was rich and yet had never done a hand's turn of work. He sometimes went fishing, but only for pleasure.

"That must be the man who has my father's heart," thought the boy, and he asked where the man lived.

The innkeeper told him the way, but his wife shook her head.

"Do not go there, my child," she said anxiously. "You will find nothing good there."

But the boy, who was sure that his father's heart was there, replied: "I must go. And tomorrow is the last day."

"Then rise early," said the innkeeper, "because he is setting out on a journey tomorrow."

Then the boy knew for certain that he had found the one he sought, recalling that the Devil had said to his father: "After ten years you can summon me. If you want me, I will come. But you will not want me."

Now the Devil was setting out on a journey—could this mean that the fisherman *had* summoned him, after all? This thought gave the boy fresh courage.

Next morning he got up early, before the sun appeared in the sky. He ran through the darkness in the direction the man had shown him and saw an old woman coming towards him.

"So," said the woman, "you are an early bird! And where are you going?"

"I am going to the Devil," said John.

The woman looked at him respectfully. "*You* can do that," she said, "for he is powerless over the innocent. Do you see the smoke in the distance? That is where he lives. But you must hurry, for he is going away. He does that every ten years, and today is the day."

The Devil opened the door himself when the boy knocked. He was fanning himself, as if he felt too hot.

"Come in," he said, "you are just in time, for I was going to visit someone. You look like him."

He led John to a great room, where there was a sound as if many clocks were ticking. The boy looked round and saw a hundred or more glass cases hanging against the walls. And in each of them hung a heart, still beating.

"A little hobby," said the Devil lightly. "Come and sit with me awhile: what can I do for you?"

The boy stood still and said: "You are the Devil."

Then the Devil sat down, for he suddenly knew that he had met his match.

"How do you know that?" he asked softly.

The boy's own heart was beating until it nearly choked him, but his voice was firm.

"I know it," he said, "and I want to know more. Whose are all those hearts?"

Now the Devil would never have answered this unless he had been feeling very weak himself. He was carrying the father's heart in his breast and he could not resist the child.

"Ask something else," he said.

"No. I am asking that."

The Devil struggled against a feeling he had never

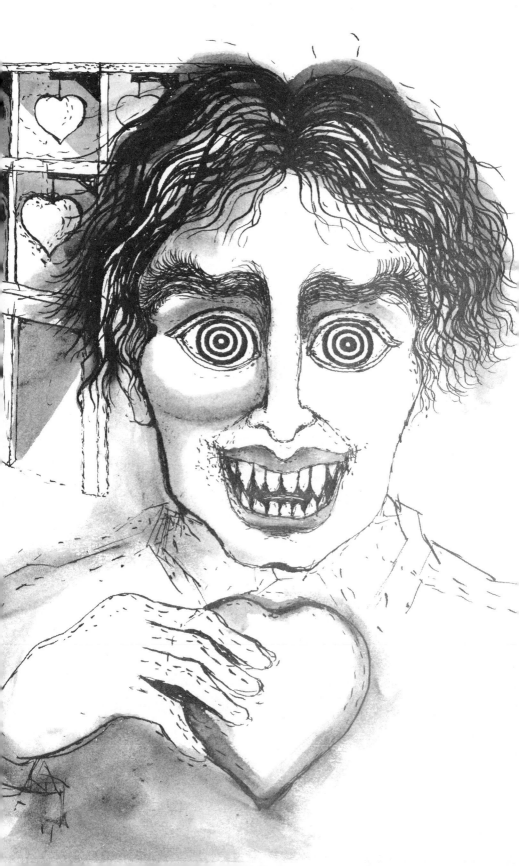

known before, and against which he was powerless.

"All right," he said, "people have sold their souls to me. Now go, for you know too much already."

"And why do you visit them after ten years?"

"I have to. If they want to, they can have their hearts back. But most of them do not. They have grown used to me. Go now, for you know too much already."

But the boy suddenly said: "Give me back my father's heart."

The Devil turned pale. "Ask for something else," he whispered.

"No. I am asking for *that*."

The Devil stared helplessly. The strange feeling was growing stronger and stronger and he could refuse the boy nothing. But suddenly he had an idea. He put his hand into his bosom, drew out the father's heart and laid it on the table. And in the same instant he drew a breath of relief, for once that heart was no longer in his breast, the child's power over him was broken. He stared at John with chilly eyes and said: "No."

But the boy had already jumped up and seized the heart from the table. He ran as fast as he could, looking back constantly, for he thought the Devil was after him. But he was wrong about that, for the Devil had not the heart to follow him. He went on sitting where he was and could not stir hand or foot.

It was already evening when the boy rushed into

his house. His father was sitting by the window.

"Father, father!" he cried breathlessly, "I have brought back your heart!"

The father looked at him indifferently, and shrugged his shoulders. Then he turned and looked out of the window as he had been doing for ten years.

The boy was dumbfounded. But suddenly he realized that his father could not help his strange aloofness, because he was still possessed of the Devil. Quickly he pushed the heart, which he had been carrying in his hands all this time, into the man's bosom and in a twinkling everything was changed!

The fisherman stood up and clasped his son in his arms. Then he looked about him and for the first time in ten years he really saw his wife and children. The tears ran down his cheeks. "How big you have grown!" he cried, "and how I love you all!" He saw the fire on the hearth and the kettle over the fire. He listened ecstatically to the wind in the chimney and the rain against the windowpanes. He heard the singing of the water boiling in the kettle and gazed in astonishment at a red geranium blooming on the window ledge. Everything was new to him and everything gave him joy. He kissed his wife on both cheeks and sat down at the table among his seven children.

"How I love you all!" he cried, again and again.

But he loved the youngest best of all, for the boy had truly stolen his heart away.

# τη∈ smiτη
# Aη∂ τη∈ ∂∈νil

*Re-told from a Welsh gypsy folktale*

*In which an old blacksmith makes himself rich and outwits the Devil. There are many versions of this story. One from Ireland has a "wee red man" instead of the Devil.*

ONCE UPON a time there was an old blacksmith who lived on the hill with his wife and mother-in-law. The only work he could do was to make ploughshares. His mother-in-law had an old mare.

One day a youth on horseback came to the smithy. "I want you to shoe my horse," he said.

"I cannot," answered the smith.

"Then give me the tools and I will do it myself."

The boy built up a huge fire. Then he cut off the horse's four legs, staunched the blood, and put them into the fire. He blew the fire for a while to make it fiercer. Then he took the legs out, put them on the anvil, beat them, and threw them on the ground. Then he took them and put them back under his horse. The old smith had been watching all this time. The youth asked what he should pay, and gave the smith a golden guinea.

146

Some days later the smith remembered his mother-in-law's mare. She needed shoeing. So he went off and brought her to the smithy. He tied the mare to the doorpost and cut off her four legs, but did not know how to staunch the bleeding! He built up a huge fire, put the four legs on it, and blew for a while as the youth had done to make the fire fiercer. But when he went to take the legs off there was nothing there: they were all burned to ashes. So he took the legless old mare and threw her over the hedge....

His wife and her mother were always quarrelling. The old blacksmith did not know how to stop them.

A couple of days later the youth on horseback returned, bringing with him two old women. "Can you make these two old women young?" he asked.

"No, I cannot."

"Will you lend me your tools? I will do it myself."

"Yes, take them."

The youth got off his horse, tossed down the two old women and bound them up. He built up a huge fire and put them on it. Then he blew and blew to make the fire fiercer. Then he took them outside, put them on the anvil, hammered them well, and put them down. They had become two young and beautiful ladies! The old smith had been watching all this time. The youth gave him a golden guinea.

A few days later it occurred to the smith that he could do the same with his wife and her mother. He bound them together and put them on a hot fire. Then he blew and blew as the youth had done. But when he

went to take them off the fire there was nothing to be
seen. They were burnt to ashes. He flung down his
hammer and went out.

"I have done it now! I have killed the old mare and
my wife and mother-in-law." He scratched his head
and couldn't think what to do. He set out from the
smithy in the deep snow without even bothering to
put a hat on.

The youth followed him. "Shall I come with you?"
he asked.

"No," said the smith. "You have nothing to do with
me."

"Do let me come with you."

The old smith relented and took him along. The boy
was bare-footed and ragged. As they went along he
told the smith: "There is a great castle near here,
where a powerful lord lives. He is ill in bed. Let's go
there."

"I can't help him," said the smith.

"Don't you say anything, then. We will both go and I
will do everything. Tell them that I am your servant."

So they went down to the castle and knocked at the
door. The butler came out.

"We have come to cure your lord," said the youth.
"Come in!"

The butler took them in to sit by the fire. He asked
what they would like to eat and drink, and they dined
very well. So well, in fact, that the old smith forgot
what they had come to do. The youth reminded him:

"Now, when the butler comes back, say that you are ready to see the lord."

So they were taken to the lord's bedroom, and the youth asked for a knife, a bowl, water and a spoon. He cut off the lord's head, and spat on his hands to staunch the blood. He put the head in the bowl and put it on the fire to boil. While it boiled he stirred with a golden spoon. Then he took the head out of the bowl and put it back on the lord's neck. The lord felt well again immediately, and gave the smith a sack of gold as a reward.

"All I want," said the youth as they set off, "is a new pair of shoes."

"No, I can't give you any. There is hardly enough gold for myself."

The youth went off and left him. . . .

So the old smith journeyed on alone, and was attacked and robbed by two men on horseback. Penniless, he went on until he heard about another lord in another castle who was also ill. He went up the castle, knocked at the door, and the butler let him in and gave him a good meal. Then the smith asked to see the lord. He asked for a knife, a bowl, water and a spoon, and cut off the lord's head. But he did not know how to staunch the blood so he had to let it bleed. He put the head into the bowl and left it on the fire to boil. While it was boiling he stirred with the golden spoon. But nothing happened, except that the head was falling to pieces and the lord was bleeding to death! Suddenly there was a knock at the door. The smith was frightened and said "No one can come in here!"

"Won't you just let a little barefoot youth in?"

The old smith opened the door and let him in, and the youth walked right up to the lord and staunched the flow of blood. Then he went to the bowl on the fire, took the golden spoon and stirred the head. It took a long time to get the head back together again: it had almost gone to rags. But at last he took it out and put it back on the lord's neck. The lord felt well at once and gave the smith two sacks of gold.

On the road the youth begged: "I want some shoes."

"All right," said the smith, "all the money is yours."

"But I don't want the money, all I want is shoes."

The youth got his shoes. . . .

They journeyed on until the youth said: "There is another great lord who lives near here. He has a wizard whom no one can beat. Let's go there. If we can beat the wizard we will win three sacks of gold."

They knocked on the castle door and spoke with the lord, and were wined and dined. Then they all went into an old house, where there was a huge pair of bellows. The lord's wizard blew up half the sea.

"Now it is your turn, my boy," said the old smith.

The youth began to blow. He blew up a great fish that drank all the sea. The wizard began to blow again. He blew up corn like rain. The youth tried and blew up birds that ate up all the corn. The wizard blew up a lot of rabbits. The youth tried again and blew up three greyhounds, which ate up all the rabbits. So he had beaten the lord's wizard and they were rewarded with three sacks of gold. . . .

The old smith hardly knew what to do with all the money. He built a new smithy, some new houses, a workshop and three inns.

One day he was doing a little work when an old woman came to the door and asked for lodging for the night. "All right," said the smith, "I can give you a bed for the night. I have no serving maid, so go on into the house, put the kettle on the fire and make yourself some tea."

The old woman ate some supper and went to bed.

In the morning she and the smith had breakfast together.

"I will grant you three wishes. What do you want?" said the old woman.

The smith answered: "I wish that any man who takes my hammer in his hand will not be able to put it down again until I say so."

"What is your second wish?"

"Do you see that old chair in the corner? I wish that any man who sits there cannot get up again until I set him free."

"All right, it shall be as you wish."

"And I wish that the man who gets into my pocket cannot get out again until I let him."

"All right," said the old woman. She thanked him and went on her way.

A few days later, when the money was getting low, a man came to the smithy. He asked the smith how he was.

"Very well. How are you?" (He recognized the man as an Evil One).

They talked for some time and eventually this man asked the smith whether he would sell himself. The smith thought for a while: "Yes," he said, "how much will you give me?"

"I will give you a sack of gold. You must come with me in five years' time. I will return to fetch you."

The Evil One left and the smith went to the inn for a drink.

Five years later the smith was doing a little work in the smithy when the Evil One arrived. "Now you must come with me."

"Very well," said the smith. "Just wait a moment. Take my hammer and do a little beating on the anvil. I'll come back when I have finished a little job."

The smith took his work home and afterwards went to one of his inns. He did some hard drinking there, came out, and went to the next inn. He had a drop there too, and came out.

While he was away the Evil One left the forge, with the hammer in his hand, and set off to look for the smith. He found him in the farthest inn, drinking with the gentry. The Devil went in, and the smith stood up to meet him.

"What are you doing with my tools?" he asked.

"Come here," said the Devil. "Remove this thing and I will give you five more years."

The old smith took the hammer and went home.

The five years passed. . . . When they were at an end the Devil walked into the smithy again. "How are you?" he asked the smith.

"Very well. How are you?"

"Now you must come away with me."

"All right. Sit down in that old chair and wait a moment while I take this home."

The Devil sat down and the smith went off to the inn and got drunk. The Devil grew tired of sitting down. He tried to get up, but could not. In the end he walked off with the chair behind him and went down to the inn. He asked whether the landlord was in.

"No," said the barmaid, "he is not here. He has gone to the next inn."

The Devil followed him to the second inn, and strode into the parlour. There he found the smith, who looked at the Devil and said: "What is that man doing with my chair?"

"Come here," said the Devil, "I want a word with you. Take this chair away and I will give you five more years."

The smith dragged the chair away and the Devil departed. The smith returned home.

The five years passed . . . and the Devil turned up again. There was no one in the workshop: the smith

was out drinking. So the Devil went to look for him. He found him in the parlour of one of his inns. The Devil sat down beside the smith and whispered in his ear.

The smith said: "I have called for ale. Turn yourself into a pound note in my pocket so that I can pay for it."

The Devil did so. The old smith drank his fill, paid his bill, and put the change into his coat pocket. Then he went home to bed. He was just falling asleep when something from below began to cry out. He got up, went downstairs and into the smithy. Then he took the pocket of his coat, held it on the anvil, seized the hammer and beat it hard.

"Let me go," screamed the Devil, "and I will leave you alone. I will never trouble you again if you will let me go."

So the old smith let him go. . . .

When the old smith finally died, he went to the Devil's door and knocked. One of the Devil's imps came out.

"Tell your master that the smith is here."
The little demon went and told his master.

"Do not let him in," said the old Devil, "or he will kill us all. Here," he continued to his serving-man, "take this wisp of straw and set fire to it to light his way up to God."

The Devil's servant did so. . . .

And this is how the old smith went up to heaven. There he sits playing his harp, and there we shall all see him one day, unless we go to the Devil instead!

# THE DEMON AND THE RABBI

## M. A. JAGENDORF

*In which a miserly Rabbi is taken to the land of Shedim (Hell) to bless a new-born baby. This is a tale taken from a collection of ancient rabbinical stories. It was translated into Spanish by a learned Jewish scholar of Morocco named Moses Edrehi. From the Spanish it was translated into two English versions, one by Thomas Keithley in 1850, and the other by L. Valentine, a little later. There are many other versions of this tale, and its theme is often found in Eastern folktales.*

THE JEWS call them Shedim or Mazzikeen. To the rest of the world they are demons, devils, creatures of another world. But they are different from any other demons or devils anywhere.

In three ways they are like angels: they can see and not be seen; they have wings and can fly; they can change to any form they want. In three ways they resemble humans; they eat and drink; they marry and have children; they die.

Once there lived a famous Rabbi, a teacher who knew all the laws, all the customs, all the traditions and proper ceremonies of the Jewish religion. Whenever there was any question of law or of any religious

157

practice, he was called. So he earned a great deal of gold—more than he could ever use. But he was a mean miser, never giving a copper to the needy. Children called him "miser" but mature folks forgave him, for they always needed him.

It happened one night, when a wild storm was raging, that there was a loud knocking at the Rabbi's door. He opened the window and in came a weird voice on a wild gust of wind and rain. It was like the screaming of an eagle or a shrill trumpet.

"Awake, thou sleeper! There is a newborn son in my house. My wife asked me to bring you to perform the proper ceremonies so that he enters the fold of Judaism."

"The night is wild as if demons were loose, and my age is great. There are those younger than I am who can administer the proper rites."

"My wife asked for you and you must come. I will pay you well."

"I do not want your gold. This day I vowed that I would do the next deed for the love of man. I will come with you and I hope your house is not far."

The Rabbi dressed and came out into the wild wind. He locked the door and put the keys under a stone. The stranger smiled at this. He was a tall man and he seemed to have heavy wings under his big cloak.

The two men set out in the driving rain, the stranger in front. His feet did not seem to touch the ground. It appeared as if the wind was carrying him along.

They walked a long time. "When do we come to your house?" the Rabbi asked.

"Soon," answered the stranger.

The Rabbi did not know where they were. To him it was all wilderness, with the rain whipping and screaming at them. A giant rock stood in their way. The tall man picked it up as if it were a hen's feather, and there, in front of them, was a big opening.

The stranger went in and the Rabbi followed. It seemed to be a strange big city. The sun shone on oddly shaped houses; people were running in all directions and singing and dancing. Often only their bodies were human. Their heads, their faces, were those of animals—snakes, bears, cocks, fish. Only the eyes were human, filled with a frightening sadness.

When they saw the Rabbi they laughed, and their laugh was like the laughing of ravens and frogs. Some screamed, "Soon you will be one of us! Soon you will be one of us!"

The Rabbi turned green with fear, and trembled. Now he knew where he was! In the land of Shedim! Mazzikeen! Demons! Devils!

He stopped and looked at the man who had led him there. His body looked like a man's, but his eyes and his mouth were like those of a beast from the other world. His face had the look of the accursed serpent that had tempted Adam and Eve. He was a Shedu—a demon, a devil.

"Come!" he said harshly. "Come!" He took hold of

the Rabbi's hand and pulled him to a big black ebony gate covered with iron grapes and green lizards and snakes.

The gate opened at a look from the Demon. They walked through many chambers until they came to one guarded by two lions with snakes' heads.

They entered a big room. In the centre stood a large bed, and in it was a lady of dazzling beauty but with a sad face. Near her lay a child wrapped in a golden coverlet.

"I have brought the man you wanted," the Demon said harshly. Then he walked out.

"I am happy you are here, but do you know where you are?" said the lady.

"I know I am in the city of demons."

"You are right. You are here because of some great wrong you have done against man. Only because of that, my husband, who is a prince among the demons, had the power to bring you here."

"I swear to heaven," the Rabbi said, "I have obeyed the laws and worshipped God according to the Bible."

"Just the same, some great wrong you have done has put you in the power of the Shedim. I am here for the same reason. I was brought from your world and married to my demon husband. They will try to keep you here, too.

"Now you must perform the proper rites over my son, and for that kind deed I will tell you how to escape from the Demon's powers."

"What must I do, Lady of Beauty?"

"Eat not, drink not, nor take any fee or reward while you are here."

The door opened and the Demon Prince, the husband of the lady, entered with a large number of friends. They were strange to behold, with faces ready to inflict evil. But the Rabbi performed the rites over the child, gave the blessings that the law prescribes, and so the child entered the fold as his mother desired.

When all the ceremonies were ended, cakes and wine were passed among those present, but the Rabbi would not touch them, saying he had made a vow not to eat that day. The Demon Prince looked at him grimly but was silent.

The Rabbi was taken to a chamber for the night, and the next morning the Demon Prince came with tempting food. "I cannot eat or drink, for today I made another vow to fast. What I desire is to go home," said the Rabbi.

The Demon looked angry at first. Then he smiled and said, "Since you desire to leave, I'll reward you for what you did for me. Come! See and choose."

"I desire no reward," the Rabbi said.

"Come and look. Perhaps you will find something that will please you." He led the Rabbi to chamber after chamber filled with silver and gold and jewels, offering them to him. The Rabbi refused. He seemed to have lost his interest in riches.

"O Rabbi," the Demon said at last, "it seems you

know me. I am the Demon who wishes to destroy you. This power I had over you obtained because of your hard heart and miserliness. Had you shown these qualities and taken my gold, I would have been able to do my evil will with you. But you did a good deed for me and I lost all my evil power over you. Now I must let you go. Come!"

The Demon Prince led him through many chambers, and at the end they came to one where many keys were hanging. The Rabbi recognized the keys to his own home. "These are the keys to my house, where I live with those I love," he said, "I do not want riches from you, O Demon Prince! I want the keys you took from me by magic."

"All these keys are from the homes of those who came into my power—but take your keys and I will take you home. Just close your eyes."

The Rabbi took his keys and closed his eyes. Then the Demon Prince spread his black wings wide open and took up the Rabbi and . . .

"Open your eyes!" he heard the Demon say. The Rabbi did, and he was in his own home with his family around him. The Demon was gone.

The Rabbi opened his heart to God, thanking Him for saving him from the Demon. Then he opened his heart and his house and his riches to all those in need. He gave alms to the poor, he cheered the hearts of the widows, and lightened the lives of orphans.

Ever after his home was free to strangers, and his

money was at the service of all in need. Everyone blessed him and the blessings multiplied a thousand-fold. Gold and avarice had no power over him, and neither did the demons.

# Tнε Οεϑιl
# Ano Oaniεl Wεbsτεr

STEPHEN VINCENT BENET

*In which Jabez Stone, dogged by bad luck, makes a contract with the Devil to sell his soul at the end of seven years in return for prosperity. All goes well until the seven years are up and Jabez does not want to give up his soul. He turns to Daniel Webster, the lawyer, for help in contesting his contract with the Devil. And this is how Daniel Webster outwits the Devil with his eloquence . . .*

## I

IT's A story they tell in the border country, where Massachusetts joins Vermont and New Hampshire.

Yes, Dan'l Webster's dead—or, at least, they buried him. But every time there's a thunderstorm around Marshfield, they say you can hear his rolling voice in the hollows of the sky. And they say that if you go to his grave and speak loud and clear, "Dan'l Webster— Dan'l Webster!" the ground'll begin to shiver and the trees begin to shake. And after a while you'll hear a deep voice saying, "Neighbour, how stands the Union?" Then you better answer that the Union stands

166

as she stood, rock-bottomed and copper-sheathed, one and indivisible, or he's liable to rear right out of the ground. At least, that's what I was told when I was a youngster.

You see, for a while, he was the biggest man in the country. He never got to be President, but he was the biggest man. There were thousands that trusted in him right next to God Almighty, and they told stories about him and all the things that belonged to him that were like the stories of patriarchs and such. They said, when he stood up to speak, stars and stripes came right out in the sky, and once he spoke against a river and made it sink into the ground. They said, when he walked the woods with his fishing rod, Killall, the trout would jump out of the streams right into his pockets, for they knew it was no use putting up a fight against him; and, when he argued a case, he could turn on the harps of the blessed and the shaking of the earth underground.

That was the kind of man he was, and his big farm up at Marshfield was suitable to him. The chickens he raised were all white meat down through the drumsticks, the cows were tended like children, and the big ram he called Goliath had horns with a curl like a morning-glory vine and could butt through an iron door. But Dan'l wasn't one of your gentlemen farmers; he knew all the ways of the land, and he'd be up by candlelight to see that the chores got done. A man with a mouth like a mastiff, a brow like a mountain and eyes like burning anthracite—that was Dan'l Webster in his prime. And the biggest case he argued never got written down in the books, for he argued it against the devil, nip and tuck and no holds barred. And this is the way I used to hear it told.

There was a man named Jabez Stone, lived at Cross Corners, New Hampshire. He wasn't a bad man to start with, but he was an unlucky man. If he planted corn, he got borers; if he planted potatoes, he got blight. He had good-enough land, but it didn't prosper him; he had a decent wife and children, but the more children he had, the less there was to feed them. If stones cropped up in his neighbour's field, boulders boiled up in his; if he had a horse with the spavins, he'd trade it for one with the staggers and give something extra. There's some folks bound to be like that, apparently. But one day Jabez got sick of the whole business.

He'd been ploughing that morning and he'd just broke the ploughshare on a rock that he could have sworn hadn't been there yesterday. And, as he stood looking at the ploughshare, the off horse began to cough—that ropy kind of cough that means sickness and horse doctors. There were two children down with the measles, his wife was ailing, and he had a whitlow on his thumb. It was about the last straw for Jabez Stone. "I vow," he said, and he looked around him kind of desperate—"I vow it's enough to make a man want to sell his soul to the devil! And I would, too, for two cents!"

Then he felt a kind of queerness come over him at

having said what he'd said; though, naturally, being a New Hampshireman, he wouldn't take it back. But all the same, when it got to be evening, and as far as he could see, no notice had been taken, he felt relieved in his mind, for he was a religious man. But notice is always taken, sooner or later, just like the Good Book says. And, sure enough, next day, about supper-time, a soft-spoken, dark-dressed stranger drove up in a handsome buggy and asked for Jabez Stone.

Well, Jabez told his family it was a lawyer, come to see him about a legacy. But he knew who it was. He didn't like the looks of the stranger, nor the way he smiled only with his teeth. They were white teeth, and plentiful—some say they were filed to a point, but I wouldn't vouch for that. And he didn't like it when the dog took one look at the stranger and ran away howling, with his tail between his legs. But having passed his word, more or less, he stuck to it, and they went out behind the barn and made their bargain. Jabez Stone had to prick his finger to sign, and the stranger lent him a silver pen. The wound healed clean, but it left a little white scar.

## II

After that, all of a sudden, things began to pick up and prosper for Jabez Stone. His cows got fat, and his horses sleek, his crops were the envy of the neighbour-hood, and lightning might strike all over the valley, but it wouldn't strike his barn. Pretty soon, he was one

of the prosperous people of the county; they asked him
to run for selectman, and he stood for it; there began
to be talk of running him for state senate. All in all,
you might say the Stone family was as happy and contented as cats in a dairy. And so they were, except for
Jabez Stone.

He'd been contented enough, the first few years. It's
a great thing when bad luck turns; it drives most other
things out of your head. True, every now and then,
especially in rainy weather, the little white scar on his
finger would give him a twinge. And once a year,
punctual as clockwork, the stranger with the handsome buggy would come driving by. But the sixth year,
the stranger lighted, and, after that, his peace was over
for Jabez Stone.

The stranger came up through the lower field,
switching his boots with a cane—they were handsome
black boots, but Jabez Stone never liked the look of
them, particularly the toes. And, after he'd passed the
time of day, he said, "Well, Mr. Stone, you're a
hummer! It's a very pretty property you've got here,
Mr. Stone."

"Well, some might favour it and others might not,"
said Jabez Stone, for he was a New Hampshireman.

"Oh, no need to decry your industry!" said the
stranger, very easy, showing his teeth in a smile.
"After all, we know what's been done, and it's been
according to contract and specifications. So when—
ahem—the mortgage falls due next year, you shouldn't

have any regrets."

"Speaking of that mortgage, mister," said Jabez
Stone, and he looked around for help to the earth and
the sky, "I'm beginning to have one or two doubts
about it."

"Doubts?" said the stranger, not quite so pleasantly.

"Why, yes," said Jabez Stone. "This being the U.S.A.,
and me always having been a religious man." He
cleared his throat and got bolder. "Yes, sir," he said,
"I'm beginning to have considerable doubts as to that
mortgage holding in court."

"There's courts and courts," said the stranger, click-
ing his teeth. "Still, we might as well have a look at the
original document." And he hauled out a big black
pocketbook, full of papers. "Sherwin, Slater, Stevens,
Stone," he muttered. "I, Jabez Stone, for a term of
seven years—Oh, it's quite in order, I think."

But Jabez Stone wasn't listening, for he saw something else flutter out of the black pocketbook. It was
something that looked like a moth, but it wasn't a
moth. And as Jabez Stone stared at it, it seemed to
speak to him in a small sort of piping voice, terribly
small and thin, but terribly human.

"Neighbour Stone!" it squeaked. "Neighbour Stone!
Help me! For God's sake, help me!"

But before Jabez could stir hand or foot, the stranger
whipped out a big bandanna handkerchief, caught the
creature in it, just like a butterfly, and started tying
up the ends of the bandanna.

"Sorry for the interruption," he said. "As I was saying—"

But Jabez Stone was shaking all over like a scared horse.

"That's Miser Stevens' voice!" he said, in a croak. "And you've got him in your handkerchief!"

The stranger looked a little embarrassed.

"Yes, I really should have transferred him to the collecting box," he said with a simper, "but there were some rather unusual specimens there and I didn't want them crowded. . . . Well, well, these little contretemps will occur."

"I don't know what you mean by contertan," said Jabez Stone, "but that was Miser Stevens' voice! And he ain't dead! You can't tell me he is! He was just as spry and mean as a woodchuck, Tuesday!"

"In the midst of life—" said the stranger, kind of pious. "Listen!" Then a bell began to toll in the valley and Jabez Stone listened, with the sweat running down his face. For he knew it was tolling for Miser Stevens and that he was dead.

"These long-standing accounts," said the stranger with a sigh; "one really hates to close them. But business is business."

He still had the bandanna in his hand, and Jabez felt sick as he saw the cloth struggle and flutter.

"Are they all as small as that?" he asked hoarsely.

"Small?" said the stranger. "Oh, I see what you mean. Why, they vary." He measured Jabez Stone with his eyes, and his teeth showed. "Don't worry, Mr. Stone," he said. "You'll go with a very good grade. I wouldn't trust you outside the collecting box. Now, a man like Dan'l Webster, of course—well, we'd have to build a special box for him, and even at that, I imagine the wing spread would astonish you. He'd certainly be a prize. I wish we could see our way clear to him. But, in your case, as I was saying—"

"Put that handkerchief away!" said Jabez Stone, and he began to beg and pray. But the best he could get at the end was a three years' extension, with conditions.

But till you make a bargain like that, you've got no idea how fast four years can run. By the last months of those years, Jabez Stone's known all over the state and there's talk of running him for governor—and it's dust and ashes in his mouth. For every day, when he gets up, he thinks, "There's one more night gone." And every night when he lies down, he thinks of the black pocketbook and the soul of Miser Stevens, and it makes him sick at heart. Till, finally, he can't bear it any longer, and, in the last days of the last year, he hitches up his horse and drives off to seek Dan'l Webster. For Dan'l was born in New Hampshire, only a few miles from Cross Corners, and it's well known that he has a particular soft spot for old neighbours.

\* \* \*

## III

It was early in the morning when he got to Marshfield, but Dan'l was up already, talking Latin to the farm hands and wrestling with the ram, Goliath, and trying out a new trotter and working up speeches to make against John C. Calhoun. But when he heard a New Hampshireman had come to see him, he dropped everything else he was doing, for that was Dan'l's way. He gave Jabez Stone a breakfast that five men couldn't eat, went into the living history of every man and woman in Cross Corners, and finally asked him how he could serve him.

Jabez Stone allowed that it was a kind of mortgage case. "Well, I haven't pleaded a mortgage case in a long time, and I don't generally plead now, except before the Supreme Court," said Dan'l, "but if I can, I'll help you."

"Then I've got hope for the first time in ten years," said Jabez Stone, and told him the details.

Dan'l walked up and down as he listened, hands behind his back, now and then asking a question, now and then plunging his eyes at the floor, as if they'd bore through it like gimlets. When Jabez had finished, Dan'l puffed out his cheeks and blew. Then he turned to Jabez Stone and a smile broke over his face like the sunrise over Monadnock.

"You've certainly given yourself the devil's own row to hoe, Neighbour Stone," he said, "but I'll take your case."

"You'll take it?" said Jabez Stone, hardly daring to believe.

"Yes," said Dan'l Webster. "I've got about seventy-five other things to do and the Missouri Compromise to straighten out, but I'll take your case. For if two New Hampshiremen aren't a match for the devil, we might as well give the country back to the Indians."

Then he shook Jabez Stone by the hand and said, "Did you come down here in a hurry?"

"Well, I admit I made time," said Jabez Stone.

"You'll go back faster," said Dan'l Webster, and he told 'em to hitch up Constitution and Constellation to the carriage. They were matched greys with one white forefoot, and they stepped like greased lightning.

Well, I won't describe how excited and pleased the whole Stone family was to have the great Dan'l Webster for a guest, when they finally got there. Jabez Stone had lost his hat on the way, blown off when they overtook the wind, but he didn't take much account of that. But after supper he sent the family off to bed, for he had most particular and private business with Mr. Webster. Mrs. Stone wanted them to sit in the front parlour, but Dan'l Webster knew front parlours and said he preferred the kitchen. So it was there they sat, waiting for the stranger, with a jug on the table between them and a bright fire on the hearth—the stranger being scheduled to show up on the stroke of midnight, according to specifications.

Well, most men wouldn't have asked for better company than Dan'l Webster and a jug. But with every tick of the clock Jabez Stone got sadder and sadder. His eyes roved round, and though he sampled the jug you could see he couldn't taste it. Finally, on the stroke of 11:30 he reached over and grabbed Dan'l Webster by the arm.

"Mr. Webster, Mr. Webster!" he said, and his voice was shaking with fear and a desperate courage. "For God's sake, Mr. Webster, harness your horses and get away from this place while you can!"

"You've brought me a long way, neighbour, to tell me you don't like my company," said Dan'l Webster, quite peaceable, pulling at the jug.

"Miserable wretch that I am!" groaned Jabez Stone. "I've brought you a devilish way, and now I see my folly. Let him take me if he wills. I don't hanker after it, I must say, but I can stand it. But you're the Union's stay and New Hampshire's pride! He mustn't get *you*, Mr. Webster! He mustn't get you!"

Dan'l Webster looked at the distracted man, all grey and shaking in the firelight, and laid a hand on his shoulder.

"I'm obliged to you, Neighbour Stone," he said gently. "It's kindly thought of. But there's a jug on the table and a case in hand. And I never left a jug or a case half finished in my life."

And just at that moment there was a sharp rap on the door.

"Ah," said Dan'l Webster, very coolly, "I thought your clock was a trifle slow, Neighbour Stone." He stepped to the door and opened it. "Come in!" he said.

The stranger came in—very dark and tall he looked in the firelight. He was carrying a box under his arm—a black, japanned box with little air holes in the lid. At the sight of the box, Jabez Stone gave a low cry and shrank into a corner of the room.

"Mr. Webster, I presume," said the stranger, very polite, but with his eyes glowing like a fox's deep in the woods.

"Attorney of record for Jabez Stone," said Dan'l Webster, but his eyes were glowing too. "Might I ask your name?"

"I've gone by a good many," said the stranger carelessly. "Perhaps Scratch will do for the evening. I'm often called that in these regions."

Then he sat down at the table and poured himself a drink from the jug. The liquor was cold in the jug, but it came steaming into the glass.

"And now," said the stranger, smiling and showing his teeth, "I shall call upon you, as a law-abiding citizen, to assist me in taking possession of my property."

Well, with that the argument began—and it went hot and heavy. At first, Jabez Stone had a flicker of hope, but when he saw Dan'l Webster being forced back at point after point, he just sat scrunched in his corner, with his eyes on that japanned box. For there wasn't any doubt as to the deed or the signature — that was the worst of it. Dan'l Webster twisted and turned and thumped his fist on the table, but he couldn't get away from that. He offered to compromise the case; the stranger wouldn't hear of it. He pointed out the property had increased in value, and state senators ought to be worth more; the stranger stuck to the letter of the law. He was a great lawyer, Dan'l Webster, but we know who's the King of Lawyers, as the Good Book tells us, and it seemed as if, for the first time, Dan'l Webster had met his match.

Finally, the stranger yawned a little. "Your spirited efforts on behalf of your client do you credit, Mr. Webster," he said, "but if you have no more arguments to adduce, I'm rather pressed for time—" and Jabez Stone shuddered.

Dan'l Webster's brow looked dark as a thundercloud. "Pressed or not, you shall not have this man!" he thundered. "Mr. Stone is an American citizen, and no American citizen may be forced into the service of a foreign prince. We fought England for that in '12 and we'll fight all hell for it again!"

"Foreign?" said the stranger. "And who calls me a foreigner?"

"Well, I never yet heard of the dev—of your claiming American citizenship," said Dan'l Webster in surprise.

"And who with better right?" said the stranger, with one of his terrible smiles. "When the first wrong was done to the first Indian, I was there. When the first slaver put out for the Congo, I stood on her deck. Am I not in your books and stories and beliefs, from the first settlements on? Am I not spoken of, still, in every church in New England? 'Tis true the North claims me for a Southerner, and the South for a Northerner, but I am neither. I am merely an honest American like yourself—and of the best descent—for, to tell the truth, Mr. Webster, though I don't like to boast of it, my name is older in this country than yours."

"Aha!" said Dan'l Webster, with the veins standing out in his forehead. "Then I stand on the Constitution! I demand a trial for my client!"

"The case is hardly one for an ordinary court," said the stranger, his eyes flickering. "And, indeed, the lateness of the hour—"

"Let it be any court you choose, if it is an American judge and an American jury!" said Dan'l Webster in his pride. "Let it be the quick or the dead; I'll abide the issue!"

"You have said it," said the stranger, and pointed his finger at the door. And with that, and all of a sudden, there was a rushing of wind outside and a noise of footsteps. They came, clear and distinct, through the night. And yet, they were not like the footsteps of living men.

"In God's name, who comes by so late?" cried Jabez

Stone, in an ague of fear.

"The jury Mr. Webster demands," said the stranger, sipping at his boiling glass. "You must pardon the rough appearance of one or two; they will have come a long way."

## IV

And with that the fire burned blue and the door blew open and twelve men entered, one by one.

If Jabez Stone had been sick with terror before, he was blind with terror now. For there was Walter Butler, the loyalist, who spread fire and horror through the Mohawk Valley in the times of the Revolution; and there was Simon Girty, the renegade, who saw white men burned at the stake and whooped with the Indians to see them burn. His eyes were green, like a catamount's, and the stains on his hunting shirt did not come from the blood of a deer. King Philip was there, wild and proud as he had been in life, with the great gash in his head that gave him his death wound, and cruel Governor Dale, who broke men on the wheel. There was Morton of Merry Mount, who so vexed the Plymouth Colony, with his flushed, loose, handsome face and his hate of the godly. There was Teach, the bloody pirate, with his black beard curling on his breast. The Reverend John Smeet, with his strangler's hands and his Geneva gown, walked as daintily as he had to the gallows. The red print of the rope was still around his neck, but he carried a perfumed handkerchief in one hand. One and all, they came into the room with the fires of hell still upon them, and the stranger named their names and their deed as they came, till the tale of twelve was told. Yet the stranger had told the truth—they had all played a part in America.

"Are you satisfied with the jury, Mr. Webster?" said the stranger mockingly, when they had taken their places.

The sweat stood upon Dan'l Webster's brow, but his voice was clear.

"Quite satisfied," he said. "Though I miss General Arnold from the company."

"Benedict Arnold is engaged upon other business," said the stranger, with a glower. "Ah, you asked for a justice, I believe."

He pointed his finger once more, and a tall man, soberly clad in Puritan garb, with the burning gaze of the fanatic, stalked into the room and took his judge's place.

"Justice Hathorne is a jurist of experience," said the stranger. "He presided at certain witch trials once held in Salem. There were others who repented of the business later, but not he."

"Repent of such notable wonders and under-takings?" said the stern old justice. "Nay, hang them —hang them all!" And he muttered to himself in a way that struck ice into the soul of Jabez Stone.

Then the trial began, and, as you might expect, it didn't look anyways good for the defence. And Jabez

Contract

I hereby agree
that I will exchange
my soul with the
Devil after a period
of seven years. In
exchange I will
receive extreme
prosperity for my
wife's family farm.

Signed
Jabez Stone

Stone didn't make much of a witness in his own behalf. He took one look at Simon Girty and screeched, and they had to put him back in his corner in a kind of swoon.

It didn't halt the trial, though; the trial went on, as trials do. Dan'l Webster had faced some hard juries and hanging judges in his time, but this was the hardest he'd ever faced, and he knew it. They sat there with a kind of glitter in their eyes, and the stranger's smooth voice went on and on. Every time he'd raise an objection, it'd be "Objection sustained," but whenever Dan'l objected, it'd be "Objection denied." Well, you couldn't expect fair play from a fellow like this Mr. Scratch.

It got to Dan'l in the end, and he began to heat, like iron in the forge. When he got up to speak he was going to flay that stranger with every trick known to the law, and the judge and jury too. He didn't care if it was contempt of court or what would happen to him for it. He didn't care any more what happened to Jabez Stone. He just got madder and madder, thinking of what he'd say. And yet, curiously enough, the more he thought about it, the less he was able to arrange his speech in his mind.

Till, finally, it was time for him to get up on his feet, and he did so, all ready to bust out with lightnings and denunciations. But before he started he looked over the judge and jury for a moment, such being his custom. And he noticed the glitter in their eyes was twice as strong as before, and they all leaned forward. Like hounds just before they get the fox, they looked, and the blue mist of evil in the room thickened as he watched them. Then he saw what he'd been about to do, and he wiped his forehead, as a man might who's just escaped falling into a pit in the dark.

For it was him they'd come for, not only Jabez Stone. He read it in the glitter of their eyes and in the way the stranger hid his mouth with one hand. And if he fought them with their own weapons, he'd fall into their power; he knew that, though he couldn't have told you how. It was his own anger and horror that burned in their eyes; and he'd have to wipe that out or the case was lost. He stood there for a moment, his black eyes burning like anthracite. And then he began to speak.

He started off in a low voice, though you could hear every word. They say he could call on the harps of the blessed when he chose. And this was just as simple and easy as a man could talk. But he didn't start out by condemning or reviling. He was talking about the things that makes a country a country, and a man a man.

And he began with the simple things that everybody's known and felt—the freshness of a fine morning when you're young, and the taste of food when you're hungry, and the new day that's every day when you're a child. He took them up and he turned them in his hands. They were good things for any man. But without freedom, they sickened. And when he talked of those enslaved, and the sorrows of slavery, his voice got like a big bell. It wasn't a spread-eagle speech, but he made you see it. He admitted all the wrong that had ever been done. But he showed how, out of the wrong and the right, the suffering and the starvations, something new had come. And everybody had played a part in it, even the traitors.

Then he turned to Jabez Stone and showed him as he was—an ordinary man who'd had hard luck and wanted to change it. And, because he'd wanted to change it, now he was going to be punished for all eternity. And yet there was good in Jabez Stone, and he showed that good. He was hard and mean, in some ways, but he was a man. There was sadness in being a man, but it was a proud thing too. And he showed what the pride of it was till you couldn't help feeling it. Yes, even in hell, if a man was a man, you'd know it. And he wasn't pleading for any one person any more, though his voice rang like an organ. He was telling the story and the failures and the endless journey of mankind. They got tricked and trapped and bamboozled, but it was a great journey. And no demon that was ever foaled could know the inwardness of it—it took a man to do that.

## V

The fire began to die on the hearth and the wind before morning to blow. The light was getting grey in the room when Dan'l Webster finished. And his words came back at the end to New Hampshire ground, and the one spot of land that each man loves and clings to. He painted a picture of that, and to each one of that jury he spoke of things long forgotten. For his voice could search the heart, and that was his gift and strength. And to one, his voice was like the forest and its secrecy, and to another like the sea and the storms of the sea; and one heard the cry of his lost nation in it, and another saw a little harmless scene he hadn't remembered for years. But each saw something. And when Dan'l Webster finished he didn't know whether or not he'd saved Jabez Stone. But he knew he'd done a miracle. For the glitter was gone from the eyes of judge and jury, and, for the moment, they were men again, and knew they were men.

"The defence rests," said Dan'l Webster, and stood there like a mountain. His ears were still ringing with his speech, and he didn't hear anything else till he heard Judge Hathorne say, "The jury will retire to consider its verdict."

Walter Butler rose in his place and his face had a dark, gay pride on it.

"The jury has considered its verdict," he said, and looked the stranger full in the eye. "We find for the defendant, Jabez Stone."

With that, the smile left the stranger's face, but Walter Butler did not flinch.

"Perhaps 'tis not strictly in accordance with the

evidence," he said, "but even the damned may salute the eloquence of Mr. Webster."

With that, the long crow of a rooster split the grey morning sky, and judge and jury were gone from the room like a puff of smoke and as if they had never been there. The stranger turned to Dan'l Webster, smiling wryly. "Major Butler was always a bold man," he said. "I had not thought him quite so bold. Nevertheless, my congratulations, as between two gentlemen."

"I'll have that paper first, if you please," said Dan'l Webster, and he took it and tore it into four pieces. It was queerly warm to the touch. "And now," he said, "I'll have you!" and his hand came down like a bear trap on the stranger's arm. For he knew that once you had bested anybody like Mr. Scratch in fair fight, his power on you was gone. And he could see that Mr. Scratch knew it too.

The stranger twisted and wriggled, but he couldn't get out of that grip. "Come, come, Mr. Webster," he said smiling palely. "This sort of thing is ridic—ouch! —is ridiculous. If you're worried about the costs of the case, naturally, I'd be glad to pay—"

"And so you shall!" said Dan'l Webster, shaking him till his teeth rattled. "For you'll sit right down at that table and draw up a document, promising never to bother Jabez Stone nor his heirs or assigns nor any other New Hampshireman till doomsday! For any hades we want to raise in this state, we can raise ourselves, without assistance from strangers."

"Ouch!" said the stranger. "Ouch! Well, they never did run very big to the barrel, but—ouch!—I agree!"

So he sat down and drew up the document. But Dan'l Webster kept his hand on his coat collar all the time.

"And, now, may I go?" said the stranger, quite humble, when Dan'l'd seen the document was in proper and legal form.

"Go?" said Dan'l, giving him another shake. "I'm still trying to figure out what I'll do with *you*. For you've settled the costs of the case, but you haven't settled with me. I think I'll take you back to Marsh-field," he said, kind of reflective. "I've got a ram there named Goliath that can butt through an iron door. I'd kind of like to turn you loose in his field and see what he'd do."

Well, with that the stranger began to beg and to plead. And he begged and he pled so humble that finally, Dan'l, who was naturally kind-hearted, agreed to let him go. The stranger seemed terribly grateful for that and said, just to show they were friends, he'd tell Dan'l's fortune before leaving. So Dan'l agreed to that, though he didn't take much stock in fortune-tellers ordinarily, and held out his hand.

But, naturally, the stranger was a little different. Well, he pried and he peered at the lines in Dan'l's hands. And he told him one thing and another that was quite remarkable. But they were all in the past.

"Yes, all that's true, and it happened," said Dan'l

Webster. "But what's to come in the future?"

The stranger grinned, kind of happily, and shook his head. "The future's not as you think it," he said. "It's dark. You have a great ambition, Mr. Webster."

"I have," said Dan'l firmly, for everybody knew he wanted to be president.

"It seems almost within your grasp," said the stranger, "but you will not attain it. Lesser men will be made president and you will be passed over."

"And, if I am, I'll still be Dan'l Webster," said Dan'l. "Say on."

"You have two strong sons," said the stranger, shaking his head. "You look to found a line. But each will die in war and neither reach greatness."

"Live or die, they are still my sons," said Dan'l Webster. "Say on."

"You have made great speeches," said the stranger. "You will make more."

"Ah," said Dan'l Webster.

"But the last great speech you make will turn many of your own against you," said the stranger. "They will call you Ichabod; they will call you by other names. Even in New England some will say you have turned your coat and sold your country, and their voices will be loud against you till you die."

"So it is an honest speech, it does not matter what men say," said Dan'l Webster. Then he looked at the stranger and their glances locked.

"One question," he said. "I have fought for the

Union all my life. Will I see that fight won against those who would tear it apart?"

"Not while you live," said the stranger, grimly. "but it will be won. And after you are dead, there are thousands who will fight for your cause, because of words that you spoke."

"Why, then, you long-barreled, slab-sided, lantern-jawed, fortune-telling note shaver!" said Dan'l Webster, with a great roar of laughter, "be off with you to your own place before I put my mark on you! For, by the thirteen original colonies, I'd go to the Pit itself to save the Union!"

And with that he drew back his foot for a kick that would have stunned a horse. It was only the tip of his shoe that caught the stranger, but he went flying out the door with his collecting box under his arm.

"And now," said Dan'l Webster, seeing Jabez Stone beginning to rouse from his swoon, "let's see what's left in the jug, for it's dry work talking all night. I hope there's pie for breakfast, Neighbour Stone."

But they say that whenever the devil comes near Marshfield, even now, he gives it a wide berth. And he hasn't been seen in the state of New Hampshire from that day to this. I'm not talking about Massachusetts or Vermont.

# WITCHES' HOLLOW

### H. P. LOVECRAFT
### AND
### AUGUST DERLETH

*In which a school teacher at a remote country school in New England is disturbed by the strange behaviour of one of his pupils. Andrew Potter seems to respond to some stimulus beyond the apprehension of an ordinary person's senses, reacting as if someone had called to him, in the same way as an animal hearing sounds beyond the pitch-level of the human ear. Determined to find out why Andrew makes so little effort in school, the teacher decides to visit his parents at their remote farm in Witches' Hollow. The road to the farm is shaded by strange, deformed trees, and the house stands in a kind of twilight, deserted and forbidding. But most disturbing of all is the chilling, hostile welcome he receives . . .*

DISTRICT SCHOOL number seven stood on the very edge of that wild country which lies west of Arkham. It stood in a little grove of trees, chiefly oaks and elms with one or two maples; in one direction the road led to Arkham, in the other it dwindled away into the wild,

192

wooded country which always looms darkly on that western horizon. It presented a warmly attractive appearance to me when first I saw it on my arrival as the new teacher early in September, 1920, though it had no distinguishing architectural feature and was in every respect the replica of thousands of country schools scattered throughout New England, a compact, conservative building painted white, so that it shone forth from among the trees in the midst of which it stood.

It was an old building at that time, and no doubt has since been abandoned or torn down. The school district has now been consolidated, but at that time it supported this school in somewhat niggardly a manner, skimping and saving on every necessity. Its standard readers, when I came there to teach, were still *McGuffey's Eclectic Readers*, in editions published before the turn of the century. My pupils added up to twenty-seven. There were Allens and Whateleys and Perkinses, Dunlocks and Abbotts and Talbots— and there was Andrew Potter.

I cannot now recall the precise circumstances of my especial notice of Andrew Potter. He was a large boy for his age, very dark of mien, with haunting eyes and a shock of tousled black hair. His eyes brooded upon me with a kind of different quality which at first challenged me but ultimately left me strangely uneasy. He was in the fifth grade, and it did not take me long to discover that he could very easily advance into the seventh or eighth, but made no effort to do so. He seemed to have only a casual tolerance for his schoolmates, and for their part, they respected him, but not out of affection so much as what struck me as fear. Very soon thereafter, I began to understand that this strange lad held for me the same kind of amused tolerance that he held for his schoolmates. Perhaps it was inevitable that the challenge of this pupil should lead me to watch him as surreptitiously as I could, and as the circumstances of teaching a one-room school permitted. As a result, I became aware of a vaguely disquieting fact; from time to time, Andrew Potter responded to some stimulus beyond the apprehension of my senses, reacting precisely as if someone had called to him, sitting up, growing alert, and wearing the air of someone listening to sounds beyond my own hearing, in the same attitude assumed by animals hearing sounds beyond the pitch-levels of the human ear.

My curiosity quickened by this time, I took the first opportunity to ask about him. One of the eighth-grade boys, Wilbur Dunlock, was in the habit on occasion of staying after school and helping with the cursory cleaning that the room needed.

"Wilbur," I said to him late one afternoon, "I notice you don't seem to pay much attention to Andrew Potter, none of you. Why?"

He looked at me, a little distrustfully, and pondered

his answer before he shrugged and replied. "He's not like us."

"In what way?"

He shook his head. "He don't care if we let him play with us or not. He don't want to."

He seemed reluctant to talk, but by dint of repeated questions I drew from him certain spare information. The Potters lived deep in the hills to the west along an all but abandoned branch of the main road that led through the hills. Their farm stood in a little valley locally known as Witches' Hollow which Wilbur described as "a bad place." There were only four of them—Andrew, an older sister, and their parents. They did not "mix" with other people of the district, not even with the Dunlocks, who were their nearest neighbours, living but half a mile from the school itself, and thus, perhaps, four miles from Witches' Hollow, with woods separating the two farms.

More than this he could not—or would not—say.

About a week later, I asked Andrew Potter to remain after school. He offered no objection, appearing to take my request as a matter of course. As soon as the other children had gone, he came up to my desk and stood there waiting, his dark eyes fixed expectantly on me, and just the shadow of a smile on his full lips.

"I've been studying your grades, Andrew," I said, "and it seems to me that with only a little effort you could skip into the sixth—perhaps even the seventh—grade. Wouldn't you like to make that effort?"

He shrugged.

"What do you intend to do when you get out of school?"

He shrugged again.

"Are you going to high school in Arkham?"

He considered me with eyes that seemed suddenly piercing in their keenness, all lethargy gone. "Mr. Williams, I'm here because there's a law says I have to be," he answered. "But there's no law says I have to go to high school."

"But aren't you interested?" I pressed him.

"What I'm interested in doesn't matter. It's what my folks want that counts."

"Well, I'm going to talk to them," I decided on the moment. "Come along, I'll take you home."

For a moment something like alarm sprang into his expression, but in seconds it diminished and gave way to that air of watchful lethargy so typical of him. He shrugged and stood waiting while I slipped my books and papers into the schoolbag I habitually carried. Then he walked docilely to the car with me and got in, looking at me with a smile that could only be described as superior.

We rode through the woods in silence, which suited the mood that came upon me as soon as we had entered the hills, for the trees pressed close upon the road, and the deeper we went, the darker grew the wood, perhaps as much because of the lateness of that October day as because of the thickening of the trees. From relatively open glades, we plunged into an ancient wood, and when at last we turned down the sideroad—little more than a lane—to which Andrew silently pointed, I found that I was driving through a growth of very old and strangely deformed trees. I had to proceed with caution; the road was so little used that underbrush crowded upon it from both sides, and, oddly, I recognized little of it, for all my studies in botany, though once I thought I saw saxifrage, curiously mutated. I drove abruptly, without warning, into the yard before the Potter house.

The sun was now lost behind the wall of trees, and the house stood in a kind of twilight. Beyond it stretched a few fields, strung out up the valley; in one, there were cornshocks, in another stubble, in yet another pumpkins. The house itself was forbidding, low to the ground, with half a second storey, gambrel-roofed, with shuttered windows, and the outbuildings stood gaunt and stark, looking as if they had never been used. The entire farm looked deserted; the only sign of life was in a few chickens that scratched at the earth behind the house.

Had it not been that the lane along which we had travelled ended here, I would have doubted that we had reached the Potter house. Andrew flashed a glance at me, as if he sought some expression on my face to convey to him what I thought. Then he jumped lightly from the car, leaving me to follow.

He went into the house ahead of me. I heard him announce me.

"Brought the teacher. Mr. Williams."

There was no answer.

Then abruptly I was in the room, lit only by an old-fashioned kerosene lamp, and there were the other three Potters—the father, a tall, stoop-shouldered man, grizzled and greying, who could not have been more than forty but looked much, much older, not so much physically as psychically—the mother, an almost obscenely fat woman—and the girl, slender, tall and with that same air of watchful waiting that I had noticed in Andrew.

Andrew made the brief introductions, and the four of them stood or sat, waiting upon what I had to say, and somewhat uncomfortably suggesting in their attitudes that I say it and get out.

"I wanted to talk to you about Andrew," I said, "he shows great promise, and he could be moved up a grade or two if he'd study a little more."

My words were not welcomed.

"I believe he's smart enough for eighth grade," I went on, and stopped.

"If he 'uz in eighth grade," said his father, "he'd be havin' to go to high school 'fore he 'uz old enough to git outa goin' to school. That's the law. They told me."

I could not help thinking of what Wilbur Dunlock had told me of the reclusiveness of the Potters, and as I listened to the elder Potter, and thought of what I had heard, I was suddenly aware of a kind of tension among them, and a subtle alteration in their attitude. The moment the father stopped talking, there was a singular harmony of attitude—all four of them seemed to be listening to some inner voice, and I doubt that they heard my protest at all.

"You can't expect a boy as smart as Andrew just to come back here," I said.

"Here's good enough," said old Potter. "Besides, he's ours. And don't ye go talkin' 'bout us now, Mr. Williams."

He spoke with so latently menacing an undercurrent in his voice that I was taken aback. At the same time I was increasingly aware of a miasma of hostility, not proceeding so much from any or all four of them, as from the house and its setting themselves.

"Thank you," I said. "I'll be going."

I turned and went out, Andrew at my heels.

Outside, Andrew said softly, "You shouldn't be talking about us, Mr. Williams. Pa gets mad when he finds out. You talked to Wilbur Dunlock."

I was arrested at getting into the car. With one foot on the running board, I turned. "Did he say so?" I asked.

He shook his head. "You did, Mr. Williams," he said, and backed away. "It's not what he thinks, but what he might do."

Before I could speak again, he had darted into the house.

For a moment I stood undecided. But my decision was made for me. Suddenly, in the twilight, the house seemed to burgeon with menace, and all the surrounding woods seemed to stand waiting but to bend upon me. Indeed, I was aware of a rustling, like the whispering of wind, in all the wood, though no wind stirred, and from the house itself came a malevolence like the blow of a fist. I got into the car and drove away, with that impression of malignance at my back like the hot breath of a ravaging pursuer.

I reached my room in Arkham at last, badly shaken. Seen in retrospect, I had undergone an unsettling psychic experience; there was no other explanation for it. I had the unavoidable conviction that, however blindly, I had thrust myself into far deeper waters than I knew, and the very unexpectedness of the experience made it the more chilling. I could not eat for the wonder of what went on in that house in Witches' Hollow, of what it was that bound the family together, chaining them to that place, preventing a promising lad like Andrew Potter even from the most fleeting wish to leave that dark valley and go out into a brighter world.

I lay for most of that night, sleepless, filled with a nameless dread for which all explanation eluded me, and when I slept at last my sleep was filled with hideously disturbing dreams, in which beings far beyond my mundane imagination held the stage, and cataclysmic events of the utmost terror and horror took place. And when I rose next morning, I felt that somehow I had touched upon a world totally alien to my kind.

I reached the school early that morning, but Wilbur Dunlock was there before me. His eyes met mine with sad reproach. I could not imagine what had happened to disturb this usually friendly pupil.

"You shouldn't a told Andrew Potter we talked about him," he said with a kind of unhappy resignation.

"I didn't, Wilbur."

"I know *I* didn't. So you must have," he said. And then, "Six of our cows got killed last night, and the shed where they were was crushed down on 'em."

I was momentarily too startled to reply. "A sudden windstorm," I began, but he cut me off.

"Weren't no wind last night, Mr. Williams. And the cows were *smashed*."

"You surely cannot think that Potters had anything to do with this, Wilbur," I cried.

He gave me a weary look—the look of one who *knows*, meeting the glance of one who should know but cannot understand, and said nothing more.

This was even more upsetting than my experience of the previous evening. He at least was convinced that there was a connection between our conversation about the Potter family and the Dunlocks' loss of half a dozen cows. And he was convinced with so deep a conviction that I knew without trying that nothing I could say would shake it.

When Andrew Potter came in, I looked in vain for any sign that anything out of the ordinary had taken place since last I had seen him.

Somehow I got through that day. Immediately after the close of the school session, I hastened into Arkham and went to the office of the Arkham *Gazette*, the editor of which had been kind enough, as a member of the local District Board of Education, to find my room for me. He was an elderly man, almost seventy, and might presumably know what I wanted to find out.

My appearance must have conveyed something of my agitation, for when I walked into his office, his eyebrows lifted, and he said, "What's got your dander up, Mr. Williams?"

I made some attempt to dissemble, since I could put my hand upon nothing tangible, and, viewed in the cold light of day, what I might have said would have sounded almost hysterical to an impartial listener. I said only, "I'd like to know something about a Potter family that lives in Witches' Hollow, west of the school."

He gave me an enigmatic glance. "Never heard of old Wizard Potter?" he asked. And, before I could answer, he went on, "No, of course, you're from Brattleboro. We could hardly expect Vermonters to know about what goes on in the Massachusetts back country. He lived there first. An old man when I first knew him. And these Potters were distant relatives, lived in Upper Michigan, inherited the property and came to live there when Wizard Potter died."

"But what do you know about them?" I persisted.

"Nothing but what everybody else knows," he said. "When they came, they were nice friendly people. Now they talk to nobody, seldom come out—and there's all that talk about missing animals from the farms in the district. The people tie that all up."

Thus begun, I questioned him at length.

I listened to a bewildering enigma of half-told tales, hints, legends and lore utterly beyond my comprehension. What seemed to be incontrovertible was a distant cousinship between Wizard Potter—a true devil!—and one Wizard Whateley of nearby Dunwich—"a bad lot," the editor called him; the solitary way of life of old Wizard Potter, and the incredible length of time he had lived; the fact that people generally shunned Witches' Hollow. What seemed to be sheer fantasy was the superstitious lore—that Wizard Potter had "called something down from the sky, and it lived with him or in him until he died";—that a late traveller, found in a dying state along the main road, had gasped out something about "that thing with the feelers—slimy, rubbery thing with the suckers on its feelers" that came out of the woods and attacked him—and a good deal more of the same kind of lore.

When he finished, the editor scribbled a note to the librarian at Miskatonic University in Arkham, and handed it to me. "Tell him to let you look at that book.

You may learn something." He shrugged. "And you may not. Young people now-days take the world with a lot of salt."

I went supperless to pursue my search for the special knowledge I felt I needed, if I were to save Andrew Potter for a better life. For it was this rather than the satisfaction of my curiosity that impelled me. I made my way to the library of Miskatonic University, looked up the librarian, and handed him the editor's note.

The old man gave me a sharp look, said, "Wait here, Mr. Williams," and went off with a ring of keys. So the book, whatever it was, was kept under lock and key.

I waited for what seemed an interminable time. I was now beginning to feel some hunger, and to question my unseemly haste—and yet I felt that there was little time to be lost, though I could not define the catastrophe I hoped to avert. Finally the librarian came, bearing an ancient tome, and brought it around and to a table within his range of vision. The book's title was in Latin—*Necronomicon*—though its author was evidently an Arabian, *Abdul Alhazred*, and its text was in somewhat archaic English.

I began to read with interest which soon turned to complete bewilderment. The book evidently concerned ancient, alien races, invaders of earth, great mythical beings called Ancient Ones and Elder Gods, with outlandish names like Cthulhu and Hastur, Shub-Niggurath and Azathoth, Dagon and Ithaqua and

Wendigo and Cthugha, all involved in some kind of plan to dominate earth and served by some of its peoples—the Tcho-Tcho, and the Deep Ones, and the like. It was a book filled with cabalistic lore, incantations, and what purported to be an account of a great interplanetary battle between the Elder Gods and the Ancient Ones and of the survival of cults and servitors in isolated and remote places on our planet as well as on sister planets. What this rigmarole had to do with my immediate problem, with the ingrown and strange Potter family and their longing for solitude and their anti-social way of life, was completely beyond me.

How long I would have gone on reading, I do not know. I was interrupted presently by the awareness of being studied by a stranger, who stood not far from me with his eyes moving from the book I was busy reading to me. Having caught my eye, he made so bold as to come over to my side.

"Forgive me," he said, "but what in this book interests a country school teacher?"

"I wonder now myself," I said.

He introduced himself as Professor Martin Keane. "I may say, sir," he added, "that I know this book practically by heart."

"A farrago of superstition."

"Do you think so?"

"Emphatically."

"You have lost the quality of wonder, Mr. Williams. Tell me, if you will, what brought you to this book?"

I hesitated, but Professor Keane's personality was persuasive and inspired confidence.

"Let us walk, if you don't mind," I said.

He nodded.

I returned the book to the librarian, and joined my new-found friend. Haltingly, as clearly as I could, I told him about Andrew Potter, the house in Witches' Hollow, my strange psychic experience,—even the curious coincidence of Dunlocks' cows. To all this he listened without interruption, indeed, with a singular absorption. I explained at last that my motive in looking into the background of Witches' Hollow was solely to do something for my pupil.

"A little research," he said, "would have informed you that many strange events have taken place in such remote places as Dunwich and Innsmouth—even Arkhan and Witches' Hollow," he said when I had finished. "Look around you at these ancient houses with their shuttered rooms and ill-lit fanlights. How many strange events have taken place under those gambrel roofs! We shall never know. But let us put aside the question of belief! One may not need to see the embodiment of evil to believe in it, Mr. Williams. I should like to be of some small service to the boy in this matter. May I?"

"By all means!"

"It may be perilous—to you as well as to him."

"I am not concerned about myself."

"But I assure you, it cannot be any more perilous to

the boy than his present position. Even death for him is less perilous."

"You speak in riddles, Professor."

"Let it be better so, Mr. Williams. But come—we are at my residence. Pray come in."

We went into one of those ancient houses of which Professor Keane had spoken. I walked into the musty past, for the rooms were filled with books and all manner of antiquities. My host took me into what was evidently his sitting room, swept a chair clear of books, and invited me to wait while he busied himself on the second floor.

He was not, however, gone very long—not even long enough for me to assimilate the curious atmosphere of the room in which I waited. When he came back he carried what I saw at once were objects of stone, roughly in the shape of five-pointed stars. He put five of them into my hands.

"Tomorrow after school—if the Potter boy is there— you must contrive to touch him with one of these, and keep it fixed upon him," said my host. "There are two other conditions. You must keep one of these at least on your person at all times, and you must keep all thought of the stone and what you are about to do out of your mind. These beings have a telepathic sense— an ability to read your thoughts."

Startled, I recalled Andrew's charging me with having talked about them with Wilbur Dunlock.

"Should I not know what these are?" I asked.

"If you can abate your doubts for the time being,"
my host answered with a grim smile. "These stones are
among the thousands bearing the Seal of R'lyeh which
closed the prisons of the Ancient Ones. They are the
seals of the Elder Gods."

"Professor Keane, the age of superstition is past,"
I protested.

"Mr. Williams—the wonder of life and its mysteries
is never past," he retorted. "If the stone has no meaning, it has no power. If it has no power, it cannot affect
young Potter. And it cannot protect you."

"From what?"

"From the power behind the malignance you felt at
the house in Witches' Hollow," he answered. "Or was
this also superstition?" He smiled. "You need not
answer. I know your answer. If something happens
when you put the stone upon the boy, he cannot be
allowed to go back home. You must bring him here to
me. Are you agreed?"

"Agreed," I answered.

That next day was interminable, not only because of
the imminence of crisis, but because it was extremely
difficult to keep my mind blank before the inquiring
gaze of Andrew Potter. Moreover, I was conscious as
never before of the wall of pulsing malignance at my
back, emanating from the wild country there, a tangible menace hidden in a pocket of the dark hills. But
the hours passed, however slowly, and just before

dismissal I asked Andrew Potter to wait after the others had gone.

And again he assented with that casual air tantamount almost to insolence, so that I was compelled to ask myself whether he were worth "saving" as I thought of saving him in the depths of my mind.

But I perservered. I had hidden the stone in my car, and, once the others were gone, I asked Andrew to step outside with me.

At this point I felt both helpless and absurd. I, a college graduate, about to attempt what for me seemed inevitably the kind of mumbo-jumbo that belonged to the African wilderness. And for a few moments, as I walked stiffly from the school house toward the car I almost flagged, almost simply invited Andrew to get into the car to be driven home.

But I did not. I reached the car with Andrew at my heels, reached in, seized a stone to slip into my own pocket, seized another, and turned with lightning rapidity to press the stone to Andrew's forehead.

Whatever I expected to happen, it was not what took place.

For, at the touch of the stone, an expression of the utmost horror shone in Andrew Potter's eyes; in a trice, this gave way to poignant anguish; a great cry of terror burst from his lips. He flung his arms wide, scattering his books, wheeled as far as he could with my hold upon him, shuddered, and would have fallen, had I not caught him and lowered him, foaming at the mouth, to the ground. And then I was conscious of a great, cold wind which whirled about us and was gone, bending the grasses and the flowers, rippling the edge of the wood, and tearing away the leaves at the outer band of trees.

Driven by my own terror, I lifted Andrew Potter into the car, laid the stone on his chest, and drove as fast as I could into Arkham, seven miles away. Professor Keane was waiting, no whit surprised at my coming. And he had expected that I would bring Andrew Potter, for he had made a bed ready for him, and together we put him into it, after which Keane administered a sedative.

Then he turned to me. "Now then, there's no time to be lost. They'll come to look for him—the girl probably first. We must get back to the school-house at once."

But now the full meaning and horror of what had happened to Andrew Potter had dawned upon me, and I was so shaken that it was necessary for Keane to push me from the room and half drag me out of the house. And again, as I set down these words so long after the terrible events of that night, I find myself trembling with that apprehension and fear which seize hold of a man who comes for the first time face to face with the vast unknown and knows how puny and meaningless he is against that cosmic immensity. I knew in that moment that what I had read in that forbidden book at the Miskatonic Library was not a farrago of superstition, but the key to a hitherto unsuspected revelation perhaps far, far older than mankind in the universe. I did not dare to think of what Wizard Potter had called down from the sky.

I hardly heard Professor Keane's words as he urged me to discard my emotional reaction and think of what had happened in scientific, more clinical fashion. After all, I had now accomplished my objective— Andrew Potter was saved. But to insure it, he must be made free of the others, who would surely follow him and find him. I thought only of what waiting horror that quartet of country people from Michigan had walked into when they came to take up possession of the solitary farm in Witches' Hollow.

I drove blindly back to the school. There, at Professor Keane's behest, I put on the lights and sat with the door open to the warm night, while he concealed himself behind the building to wait upon their coming. I had to steel myself in order to blank out my mind and take up that vigil.

On the edge of night, the girl came . . .

And after she had undergone the same experience as her brother, and lay beside the desk, the star-shaped stone on her breast, their father showed up in the doorway. All was darkness now, and he carried a gun. He had no need to ask what had happened; he *knew*. He stood wordless, pointed to his daughter and the stone on her breast, and raised his gun. His inference was plain—if I did not remove the stone, he meant to shoot. Evidently this was the contingency the professor expected, for he came upon Potter from the rear and touched him with the stone.

Afterwards we waited for two hours—in vain, for Mrs. Potter.

"She isn't coming," said Professor Keane at last. "She harbours the seat of its intelligence—I had thought it would be the man. Very well—we have no choice—we must go to Witches' Hollow. These two can be left here."

We drove through the darkness, making no attempt at secrecy, for the professor said the "thing" in the house in the Hollow "knew" we were coming but could not reach us past the talisman of the stone. We went through that close-pressing forest, down the narrow lane where the queer undergrowth seemed to reach out toward us in the glow of the headlights, into the Potter yard.

The house stood dark save for a wan glow of lamplight in one room.

Professor Keane leaped from the car with his little bag of star-shaped stones, and went around sealing the house—with a stone at each of the two doors, and one at each of the windows, through one of which we could see the woman sitting at the kitchen table—stolid, watchful, *aware*, no longer dissembling, looking unlike that tittering woman I had seen in this house not long ago, but rather like some great sentient beast at bay.

When he had finished, my companion went around to the front and, by means of brush collected from the yard and piled against the door, set fire to the house, heedless of my protests.

Then he went back to the window to watch the woman, explaining that only fire could destroy the elemental force, but that he hoped, still, to save Mrs. Potter. "Perhaps you'd better not watch, Williams."

I did not heed him. Would that I had—and so spared myself the dreams that invade my sleep even yet! I stood at the window behind him and watched what went on in that room—for the smell of smoke was now permeating the house. Mrs. Potter—or what animated her gross body—started up, went awkwardly to the back door, retreated, to the window, retreated from it, and came back to the centre of the room, between the table and the wood stove, not yet fired against the coming cold. There she fell to the floor, heaving and writhing.

The room filled slowly with smoke, hazing about the yellow lamp, making the room indistinct—but not indistinct enough to conceal completely what went on in the course of that terrible struggle on the floor, where Mrs. Potter threshed about as if in mortal convulsion and slowly, half visibly, something other took shape—an incredible amorphous mass, only half glimpsed in the smoke, tentacled, shimmering, with a cold intelligence and a physical coldness that I could feel through the window. The thing rose like a cloud

above the now motionless body of Mrs. Potter, and then fell upon the stove and drained into it like vapour!

"The stove!" cried Professor Keane, and fell back.

Above us, out of the chimney, came a spreading blackness, like smoke, gathering itself briefly there. Then it hurtled like a lightning bolt aloft, into the stars, in the direction of the Hyades, back to that place from which old Wizard Potter had called it into himself, away from where it had lain in wait for the Potters to come from Upper Michigan and afford it new host on the face of earth.

We managed to get Mrs. Potter out of the house, much shrunken now, but alive.

On the remainder of that night's events there is no need to dwell—how the professor waited until fire had consumed the house to collect his store of star-shaped stones, of the reuniting of the Potter family—freed from the curse of Witches' Hollow and determined never to return to that haunted valley—of Andrew, who, when we came to waken him, was talking in his sleep of "great winds that fought and tore" and a "place by the Lake of Hali where they live in glory forever."

What it was that old Wizard Potter had called down from the stars, I lacked the courage to ask, but I knew that it touched upon secrets better left unknown to the races of men, secrets I would never have become aware of had I not chanced to take District School Number Seven, and had among my pupils the strange boy who was Andrew Potter.